Presented To

_____

From

_____

Success Leaves Clues

Success Leaves Clues

Standing on the Shoulders of the World's Greatest Thought Leaders.

Extraordinary maxims of keen insight on the achievement of success and significance in life and Business.

Daniel Gleed

SUCCESS *YOU*niversity

Coaching, Consulting and Training

Building People, Growing Leaders and Expanding Business

Copyright © 2015 Daniel Gleed

First edition, 2015

All Rights Reserved

Published in the United States of America

Cataloging -in-Publication data is on file with the library of congress.

Daniel Gleed

Success Leaves Clues

ISBN 978-0-692-38635-4

Printed in the United States of America

10 9 8 7 6 5 4 3 2 1

Cover Design by Melissa Brice at *WILDESIGN*

http://www.melbwildesign.com

For more information about special discounts for bulk
purchases please contact Success YOUniversity at
www.DanielGleed.com

I respect the man who knows distinctly what he wishes. The greater part of all mischief in the world arises from the fact that men do not sufficiently understand their own aims. They have undertaken to build a tower and spend no more labor on the foundation than would be necessary to erect a hut.

~ Johann Wolfgang von Goethe ~

In regard to negativity and exposing yourself to toxic environments, toxic people and toxic words, you wouldn't let anyone come into your living room and dump a bag of trash on your floor, so why would you let people do that to your mind?

~ Daniel Gleed ~

Great people talk about ideas, average people talk about things, small people talk about other people. And sadly, there are even smaller people who only love to talk about themselves.

~ Eleanor Roosevelt ~

DEDICATION

This book is dedicated to Jim Gleed, my father and the greatest man I've ever known.

Dad kept a 3x5 card on a clip board above his dresser and on it was a quote that he lived by.

It said:

"To be successful is to be helpful caring and constructive, to make everything and everyone you touch a little better. The best thing you have to give is yourself."

~ *Napoleon Hill* ~

My Dad lived by this quote and it is evident by all the people who loved him. He had a personal charm, a magnetism that drew people in, a charisma that everyone loved about him. People always felt at ease around him and it opened them up to be able to be deeply touched and influenced by him in the most awesome way.

Time passed by after Dad died and Mom called Columbia cleaning company to have the carpets cleaned. The guy wouldn't accept mom's money. He said in years past as an employee of Columbia cleaning, and my father's co-worker, Dad use to give him a shoulder to lean on and inspired him to be great. He said to my Mom, I'm not an employee of Columbia Cleaning anymore, "*I own the company*." Your husband changed my life forever.

This book is dedicated to you Dad, you are the greatest man I ever knew and thank you for always leading by example and for all the great memories, the great stories and the great teachings. Your life and the time spent with us is the most incredibly beautiful kaleidoscope of family history, and I speak of you in the present tense rather than the past because even though your physical presence has been stolen from us, your spirit is with us every day. Thank you for serving our country and protecting our freedom, thank you for being the greatest husband, father, grandfather, uncle and friend. Thank you for always giving us the greatest gift you could ever give.

"Your Precious Time."

I love you Dad.

Table of Contents

When you sell a man a book you don't sell just twelve ounces of paper, ink and glue - you sell him a whole new life. Love and friendship and humor and ships at sea by night - there's all heaven and earth in a book, a real book.

~ Christopher Morley~

There is power and greatness in the proper construction of words.

This book is the key to unlocking that power.

The limits of your vocabulary and your ability to use them are also the limits of your world.

"abcdefghijklmnopqrstuvwxyz"

All of the letters of the alphabet listed above can be arranged in ways that can make you laugh, make you cry, and make you experience emotions of love and hate. They can make you pause and think, and they can lead to understanding and wisdom. How you rearrange these letters is how you create your world both in business and in your personal lives.

Some people have arranged and re-arranged these letters for good and some have manipulated them for evil. Then there are the thought leaders in this book who have rearranged them to solve problems, create new ideas, inspire and empower others to greatness and put their thoughts into a form that brings meaning to life and the world around us.

The most important question at hand is......

How will you rearrange them?

This book is a quantum catalyst for sparking new ideas, creating new methods for doing things, new strategies for business, igniting new plans and programs, building stronger leadership within families and companies, and bolstering wiser entrepreneurial endeavors. It's a wealth of free advice just sitting on your desk or your night stand, ready and willing to help you without notice. It's your most loyal friend and comrade in life. Keep it handy and refer to it often.

DISCLAIMER

The trouble with quotes on the internet is that it's hard to verify their authenticity.

~ *Abraham Lincoln* ~

The quotes in this book have been gathered from many resources including the internet and the above quote illustrates perfectly what I'm trying to say. Of course, Abraham Lincoln was dead long before the dawn of the internet, therefore he could not have made the above statement. It is difficult to verify authenticity of quotes on the internet however I have gone to great lengths to make sure that appropriate credit is given.

Preface

The idea for researching and assembling a collection of the most powerful transformational quotes ever put forward, spoken by the world's most successful and most influential men and women of all time was inspired by my parents. When I was 15 years old my mom and dad put a book of quotes in my Christmas stocking. One of those quotes has always stuck with me and it went like this;

"When I was 15, my Dad was so stupid that I couldn't stand to be around him, but when I turned 20 I was amazed at how much my Dad had learned in 5 years."

Although that quote does emit an aura of humor, I will never forget how awesome my dad was, and how stupid "I" was at that time. That quote really hit home and I'm thankful that my dad let me grow through this phase without ever slapping me silly.

That book of quotes was a gift that Mom and Dad gave to me, a gift filled with wisdom that touched my life in many ways and I'm thankful that I get to pass on a similar gift to you. There are all kinds of books of quotes, for this topic, and that topic, and then there is...

"this" book of quotes that has the ability to change lives. A vault filled with real authentic jewels of wisdom passed on from the minds of the greatest thought leaders of our time and from decades and centuries before. The quotation marks have served as a vehicle to transport wisdom through the ages and continue to inspire greatness and change lives.

I have searched high and low to find the most amazing quotes that I have ever seen. This book is meant to be a higher education contained in small quotations of living energy that jolt your thought process and cause a light to pop on and shift the way that you think. A quote from Oliver Wendell Holmes Jr. says that a mind once expanded by a new experience, never returns to its original dimensions. My goal for this book is to jolt you and stretch you mentally, spiritually and emotionally to new dimensions.

Congratulations on investing in your most valuable asset, yourself! Listen to yourself as you read and hear the words throughout this book and spare yourself the hassle of finding the perfect place in your mental rolodex to file each quote that has special meaning to you. There is already a perfect pre-ordained place inside of you, patiently waiting for each of your special quotes to arrive and take seat in their new home where they will lay seemingly dormant, waiting for opportunities to express themselves when they are needed by a passionate leader such as yourself.

Leadership is a 12-inch journey from the head to the heart, and the heart is where great leaders will lead from, that is where true leaders find success and that is where the quotes in this book that you connect with will show up out of the blue and insert themselves into your conversation like it was divine intervention.

Your new knowledge is instinctively drawn into the fold as opportunities present themselves. You don't need to have quotes, knowledge or all the answers sitting on top of your head, ready at your disposal for you to enter into an interaction with others.

Just have faith, trust yourself and submit yourself to the challenge of leadership. When you step forward to lead, your knowledge and intuition will be there with you when you need them. As Michael Jordan said, "Just do it."

Speaking of quotes this is the perfect spot for one more quote. As Francis Crick, the Nobel Prize winner for his discovery of the Double Helix, said during his acceptance speech while "quoting" Sir Isaac Newton, *"**If I have seen farther than others, it is because I have stood on the shoulders of giants**."*

This book is full of Giants with great shoulders to stand on and I hope that you will stand on them often.

A

Action

The difference between successful people and everyone else is that successful people take action. And if they fail, guess what? They take a different action until they find one that works. ~ *Talayah G. Stovall, (Author of Light Bulb Moments)*

Ignorance on fire is better than knowledge on ice. ~ *Unknown*

Action creates motivation, motivation does not create action. ~ *Unknown*

Whatever you're ready for is ready for you. ~ *Mark Victor Hansen*

Thinking is easy, action is difficult. To act in accordance with one's thought is the most difficult thing in the world. ~ *Goethe*

The reality of life is that if you aren't building or working towards your own dream, it's someone else's dream you are helping to build. ~ *Joshua Schneider*

When it's obvious that goals can't be reached, don't adjust the goals, adjust the actions steps. ~ *Confucius.*

An organizations ability to learn and translate that learning into action rapidly, is the ultimate competitive advantage. ~ *Jack Welch*

Do you want to know who you are? Don't ask. Act! Action will delineate and define you. ~ *Thomas Jefferson*

It would be much better to try something and fail than to never try and spend the rest of your life focused on what-ifs. ~ *Talayah G. Stovall*

Inaction breeds doubt and fear, Action breeds confidence and courage. If you want to conquer fear, do not sit home and think about it. Go out and get busy. ~ *Dale Carnegie*

Men who try to do something and fail are infinitely better than those who try to do nothing and succeed. ~ *Lloyd Jones*

Action is the foundational key to all success ~ *Pablo Picasso*

Upon the plains of hesitation are the bleached bones of countless millions, who on the threshold of victory, sat down to wait, and in waiting they died. ~ *Unknown*

Not in his speech, not in his thoughts, I see his greatness only in his actions ~ *Hermann Hesse*

Advertising

Advertising is the greatest art form of the twentieth century. ~ *Marshal McLuhan*

The business that considers itself immune to the necessity for advertising, sooner or later finds itself immune to business. ~ *Derby Brown*

The best advertising should make you nervous about what you're not buying. ~ *Mary Wells Lawrence*

In advertising, not to be different is virtually suicidal. ~ *Bill Bernbach*

Many a small thing has been made large by the right kind of advertising. ~ *Mark Twain*

No one remembers the number of ads you run, they just remember the impression you make. ~ *Bill Bernbach*

Advertising is the science of arresting the human intelligence long enough to get money from it. ~ *Stephen Leacock*

A good advertisement is one which sells the product without drawing attention to itself. ~ *David Ogilvy*

Assumption

People prefer opinions to truth. They try to bend the world to fit their assumptions, instead of changing their assumptions to fit the world. ~ *Elizabeth C. Mock*

Most of our assumptions have outlived their usefulness. ~ *Marshall McLuhan*

The assumptions you make about someone should never be based on what you "heard." ~ *Unknown*

People prefer opinions to truth. They try to bend the world to fit their assumptions, instead of changing their assumptions to fit the world. ~ *Elizabeth C. Mock*

Assumptions are unopened windows that foolish birds fly into, and their broken bodies are evidence gathered too late. ~ *Bryan Davis*

Assumptions are the termites of relationships. You must stick to your convictions but be ready to abandon your assumptions ~ *Dennis Waitley*

Our future will be shaped by the assumptions we make about who we are and what we can be. ~ *R.M. Kanter*

To assume is to limit the mind to one way of viewing, when by nature our perceptions should be infinite. ~ *Unknown*

There are no accidents... there is only some purpose that we haven't yet understood. ~ *Deepak Chopra*

If we integrate the spoiled assumptions of our current era into our products, we will lock ourselves into a future that is literally designed to fail. ~ *David Wann*

Attitude

The greatest discovery of my generation is that human beings can alter their lives by altering their attitudes of mind. ~ *William James*

A bad attitude is like a flat tire, if you don't' change it you'll never go anywhere. ~ *Unknown*

There is little difference in people, but that little difference makes a big difference. The little difference is attitude, and the big difference is whether it is positive or negative. ~ *W. Clement Stone*

Attitude is a little thing that makes a big difference. ~ *Winston Churchill*

No one can depress you. No one can make you anxious. No one can hurt your feelings. No one can make you anything other than what you allow inside. ~ *Wayne Dyer*

Accept responsibility for your life. Know that it is you who will get you where you want to go, no one else. ~ *Les Brown*

A strong positive mental attitude will create more miracles than any wonder drug. ~ *Patricia Neal*

Think you can't or think you can – either way, you'll be right. ~ *Henry Ford*

A smile is a crooked line that sets everything else straight. ~ *Unknown*

Acknowledgment

Never underrate the importance of visibly appreciating others and their efforts. ~ *Joan Nicolo*

When we sow the seeds of recognition and appreciation, we reap greater accomplishments from people. ~ *Jack Canfield*

Rewards and recognition provide the best results when used as a communications medium to get attention, convey a message and build closer relationships over time. ~ *Unknown*

When people don't get enough recognition, they ask themselves, what am I doing this for? Nobody cares. ~ *Unknown*

According to the study by SHRM and Globoforce, more than half of the human resource managers surveyed say their front-line bosses don't say thank you enough. ~ *Wall Street Journal*

Employees who make empowered decisions should be recognized in a significant way. Feature them in the company publication. Give them a prime parking spot near the front door for a week. Throw a pizza party. By doing so you are sending a message to the rest of the workforce that empowerment is important. ~ *John Tschohl*

B

Belief

A belief is not just an idea that you possess; it is an idea that possess you. ~ *Unknown*

Magic is believing in yourself, if you can do that, you can make anything happen. ~ *Goethe*

Believe that life is worth living and your belief will help create the fact. ~ *William James*

A belief is a thought in the subconscious mind, it means to accept something as true. Thought once accepted, executes itself automatically. ~ *Joseph Murphy*

Those who don't believe in magic will never find it. ~ *Roald Dahl*

Your belief determines your action and your action determines your results, but first you have to believe. ~ *Mark Victor Hansen*

Those who can make you believe absurdities can make you commit atrocities. ~ *Voltaire*

Every mental act is composed of doubt and belief, but it is belief that is the positive. It is belief that sustains thought and holds the world together. ~ *Soeren Kierkegaard*

Remember that a wish held fervently turns into belief, and a belief held diligently becomes reality. ~ *Jim Stovall*

Behavior

Your conscious mind operates at about 126 bits per second, while your subconscious mind is 10,000 times faster. ~ *Brian E. Walsh. PhD* (Author of Unleashing Your Brilliance)

The character of the architectural forms and spaces which all people habitually encounter are powerful agencies in determining the nature of their thoughts, their emotions and their actions, however unconscious of this they may be. ~ *Hugh Ferriss*

Behavior is the mirror in which everyone shows their image. ~ *Johann Wolfgang von Goethe*

The self-image is the key to human personality and human behavior. Change the self-image and you change the personality and the behavior. ~ *Maxwell Maltz*

I think that when you get dressed in the morning, sometimes you're really making a decision about your behavior for the day. Like if you put on flipflops, you're saying: 'Hope I don't get chased today.' 'Be nice to people in sneakers. ~ *Demetri Martin*

Stress from chronically noisy environments can lead to increased feelings of helplessness. ~ *Brian E. Walsh. PhD*

People tend to raise the child inside of them rather than the child in front of them. ~ *Joe Newman*

We know what we are but not what we may be. ~ *Ophelia in Hamlet*

If you put yourself in a position where you have to stretch outside your comfort zone, then you are forced to expand your consciousness. ~ *Les Brown*

The Brain is the only organ is the body that sculpts itself from outside experience. In a sense you experience become biology. ~ *Brian E. Walsh PhD*

Don't become a mere recorder of facts but try to penetrate the mystery of their origin. ~ *Ivan Pavlov*

But behavior in the human being is sometimes a defense, a way of concealing motives and thoughts, as language can be a way of hiding your thoughts and preventing communication. ~ *Abraham Maslow*

The ABC's are attitude, behavior and communication skills. ~ *Gerald Chertavian*

Everybody experiences far more than he understands. Yet it is experience, rather than understanding, that influences behavior. ~ *Marshall McLuhan*

Because cheating is easier when we can justify our behavior, people often cheat in small amounts: We can come up with an excuse for stealing Post-It notes, but it is much more difficult to come up with an excuse for taking $10,000 from petty cash. ~ *Dan Ariely*

If your feet are flat on the floor, the area under your feet corresponds to the processing ability of your conscious mind. The floor area in the room not covered by your feet represents the power of your subconscious mind. ~ *Brian E. Walsh*

The disappearance of a sense of responsibility is the most far-reaching consequence of submission to authority. ~ *Stanley Milgram*

The greatest discovery of my generation is that human beings can alter their lives by altering their attitudes of mind. ~ *William James*

Brain

Our minds influence the key activity of the brain, which then influences everything; perception, cognition, thoughts and feelings, personal relationships; they're all a projection of you. ~ *Deepak Chopra*

The brain is a wonderful organ; it starts working the moment you get up in the morning and does not stop until you get into the office. ~ *Robert Frost*

The human brain has 100 billion neurons, each neuron connected to 10 thousand other neurons. Sitting on your shoulders is the most complicated object in the known universe. ~ *Michio Kaku*

Biology gives you a brain. Life turns it into a mind. ~ *Jeffrey Eugenides*

In comparing the capacity of computers to the capacity of the human brain, I've often wondered, where does our success come from? The answer is synthesis, the ability to combine creativity and calculation, art and science into a whole that is much greater than its parts. ~ *Garry Kasparov*

Consciousness is the basis of all life and the field of all possibilities. Its nature is to expand and unfold its full potential. The impulse to evolve is thus inherent in the very nature of life. ~ *Maharishi Mahesh Yogi*

All matter originates and exists only by virtue of a force... We must assume behind this force the existence of a conscious and intelligent Mind. This Mind is the matrix of all matter. ~ *Max Planck, Nobel Prize-winning Father of Quantum Theory*

The whole history of science has been the gradual realization that events do not happen in an arbitrary manner, but that they reflect a certain underlying order, which may or may not be divinely inspired. ~ *Stephen W. Hawking*

13

Increase your consumption of healthful fats like extra virgin olive oil, avocado, grass-fed beef, wild fish, coconut oil, nuts and seeds. At the same time, keep in mind that modified fats like hydrogenated or trans fats are the worst choices for brain health. ~ *David Perlmutter*

Learning is physical. Learning means the modification, growth, and pruning of our neurons, connections-called synapses- and neuronal networks, through experience...we are cultivating our own neuronal networks. ~ Dr. James Zull

Individuals who lead mentally stimulating lives, through education, occupation and leisure activities, have reduced risk of developing Alzheimer's symptoms. Studies suggest that they have 35-40% less risk of manifesting the disease. ~ *Dr. Yaakov Stern*

Elite performers are distinguished by the structuring of their learning process...You need to protect and optimize that practice, learning time... It is important to understand the role of emotions: they are not "bad". They are very useful signals. It is important to become aware of them to avoid being engulfed by them, and learn how to manage them. ~ *Dr. Brett Steenbarger*

What is reality? Is reality what we're seeing in our brain? Or is reality what we're seeing with our eyes? The truth is the brain does not know the difference between what it sees in its environment and what it remembers, because the same specific neurons of fire. But then it asks the question: what is reality? ~ *Joseph Dispenza*

Business Savvy

If you don't have a competitive advantage, don't compete. ~ *Jack Welch*

A critic is someone who knows the direction but can't drive the vehicle. ~ *Unknown*

Whenever you see a successful business it indicates that someday someone made a brave decision. ~ *Peter Drucker*

Before you are a leader, success is all about growing yourself, when you become a leader, success is all about growing others. ~ *Jack Welch*

Success depends on collaboration and unity. ~ *Graham Alexander*

The entrepreneur always searches for change, responds to it and exploits it as an opportunity. ~ *Peter Drucker.*

Whenever you have a grievance, only take it to somebody who can fix it. Only have conversations with people who can affect things positively. ~ *Graham Alexander*

In the end, all business operations can be reduced to three words: people, product and profits. Unless you've got a good team, you can't do much with the other two. ~ *Lee Iacocca*

Design bugs are often subtle and occur by evolution with early assumptions being forgotten, as new features or uses are added to systems. ~ *Fernando J. Corbato*

The better a man is, the more mistakes he will make, for the more new things he will try. I would never promote into a top-level job, a man who was not making mistakes, otherwise he is sure to be mediocre. ~ *Peter Drucker*

By outsourcing your customer service function, you're in danger of losing control of your company's destiny. You've abdicated your responsibility for the most important person in your business: "your customer". ~ *Graham Alexander*

Giving people self-confidence is by far the most important thing I can do. Because then they will act. ~ *Jack Welch*

Management is doing things right, leadership is doing the right things. ~ *Peter Drucker*

An organizations ability to learn, and translate that learning into action rapidly, is the ultimate competitive advantage. ~ *Jack Welch*

In times of change learners inherit the earth, while the learned find themselves beautifully equipped to deal with a world that no longer exists. *~ Jack Welch*

Encourage your staff to be candid with you. Ask their advice and listen to it. Top bananas have no monopoly on ideas. *~ David Ogilvey*

The enterprise that does not innovate, inevitably ages and declines. And in a period of rapid change such as the present ...... the decline will be fast. *~ Peter Drucker*

Recipe for success: First, make a reputation for creative genius. Second, surround yourself with partners who are better than you are. Third, leave them to get on with it. *~ David Ogilvy*

Willingness to change is a strength, even if it means plunging part of the company into total confusion for a while. *~ Jack Welch*

All organizations are perfectly aligned to get the results they get. *~ Arthur W. Jones*

My greatest strength as a consultant is to be ignorant and ask a few questions. *~ Peter Drucker*

If the rate of change on the outside, exceeds the rate of change on the inside, the end is in sight. *~ Jack Welch*

Every job is a self-portrait of the person who did it. Autograph your work with excellence. *~ Jessica Guidobono*

Resorting to lying and cheating in any business amounts to conceding defeat. *~ George Hammond*

Meetings are a symptom of bad organization, the fewer meetings the better. *~ Peter Drucker*

Success is only another form of failure if we forget what our priorities should be. *~ Harry Lloyd*

Within five years, if you're in the same business you're in now, you're going to be out of business. *~ Peter Drucker*

Genuine leadership comes from the quality of your vision and your ability to spark others into extraordinary performance. ~ *Jack Welch*

Plans are only good intentions unless they immediately degenerate into hard work. ~ *Peter Drucker*

If you can't measure it, you can't manage it. ~ *Peter Drucker*

The most important thing in communication is hearing what isn't being said. ~ *Peter Drucker*

The business enterprise has two, and only these two basic functions: Marketing and innovation. Marketing and innovation produce results, all the rest are just costs. ~ *Peter Drucker*

C

Celebrating Success

Ceremonies, celebrations, and rituals are not about the event. They are about touching the hearts and souls of every employee. ~ *Victoria Sandvig*

Celebrate what you've accomplished but raise the bar a little higher each time you succeed. ~ *Mia Hamm*

Celebrate your success and find humor in your failures. Don't take yourself so seriously. Loosen up and everyone around you will loosen up. Have fun and always show enthusiasm. When all else fails, put on a costume and sing a silly song. ~ *Sam Walton*

In my eyes, every day is a celebration, our love, business, and family is not a result, but a constant reminder why we must celebrate this success we've built out of passion. ~ *Unknown*

Champions

Champions aren't made in gyms. Champions are made from something they have deep inside them, a desire, a dream, and a vision. They have to have the skill and they must be stronger than the skill. ~ *Muhammad Ali*

Champions do not become champions when they win the event, but in the hours, weeks, months, and years they spend preparing for it. The victorious performance itself is merely the demonstration of their championship character. ~ *T. Alan Armstrong*

To be a great champion you must believe you're the best. If you're not, pretend you are. ~ *Muhammad Ali*

Hard days are the best because that's when champions are made. ~ *Gabrielle Douglas*

I'm so fast that last night I turned off the light switch and I was in bed before the room went dark. ~ *Muhammad Ali*

Float like a butterfly, sting like a bee, the hands can't hit, what the eyes can't see. ~ *Muhammad Ali*

True champions aren't always the ones that win, but they are the ones with the most guts. ~ *Ma Hamm*

If you even dream of beating me, you'd better wake up and apologize. ~ *Muhammad Ali*

For men and women who want to be champions, the mind can be as important if not more important, than any other part of the body. ~ *Gary Neville*

It is the lack of faith that makes people afraid of meeting challenges. I' believe in myself. ~ *Muhammad Ali*

Every champion was once a contender that refused to give up. ~ *Unknown*

I don't count all my sit-ups, I only start counting when it starts hurting, when I feel the pain, that's when I start counting, because that's when it really counts. ~ *Muhammad Ali*

I'm not the greatest, I'm the double greatest. Not only do I knock them out, I pick the round! ~ *Muhammad Ali*

I am the greatest, and I said that even before I knew I was. ~ *Muhammad Ali*

It's not considered bragging if you can back it up. ~ Muhammad Ali

Eat like a cave man, train like a beast. Champions are not born they are made. ~ *The Rock*

A man who views the world the same at 50 as he did at 20 has wasted 30 years of his life. ~ *Muhammad Ali*

It's not just the will to win that matters most, it's the will to prepare to win that is important. ~ *Michael Jordan*

Life is like a boxing match, defeat is declared not when you fall, but when you refuse to stand again. ~ *Muhammad Ali*

Character

People of character do the right thing, even if no one else does, not because they think it will change the world, but because they refuse to be changed by the world. ~ *Micheal Josephson*

Our character is what we do when we think no one is looking. ~ *Karl Schonhausen*

Many times, a day I realize how much my own outer and inner life is built upon the labors of my fellow men, both living and dead, and how earnestly I must exert myself in order to give in return as much as I have received from that connection. ~ *Albert Einstein*

You can tell a lot about a person by the way he or she handles three things; a rainy day, lost luggage and tangled Christmas tree lights. ~ *Maya Angelou*

Character is how you treat those who can do nothing for you. ~ *Unknown*

Weakness of attitude becomes weakness of character. ~ *Albert Einstein*

Character is like a tree and reputation like a shadow, the shadow is what we think of it, the tree is the real thing. ~ *Abraham Lincoln*

The content of your character is your choice. Day by day what you choose, what you think and what you do is who you become. ~ *Heraclitus*

A true test of character isn't how you are on your best days, but how you act on your worst days. ~ *Unknown*

When wealth is lost, nothing is lost, when health is lost, something is lost, when character is lost, all is lost. ~ *Billy Graham*

Don't mistake my kindness for weakness, I am kind to everyone, but when someone is unkind to me, weak is not what you are going to remember about me. ~ *Al Capone*

Never do anything which you would be afraid to do if it was the last hour of your life. ~ *Jonathan Edwards*

Thoughts become words, words become actions, actions become habits, habits become character and character shapes your destiny. ~ *James Allen*

If I take care of my character, my reputation will take care of itself. ~ *Dwight Lyman Moody*

The best index to a person's character is how he treats people who can't do him any good, and how he treats people who can't fight back. ~ *Abigail Van Buren*

If people refuse to look at you in a new light and they can only see for what you were, only see you for the mistakes you've made, if they don't realize that you are not your mistakes, then they have to go! ~ *Steve Maraboli*

Good character is not formed in a week or a month, it is created little by little, day by day. Protracted and patient effort is needed to develop good character ~ *Heraclitus of Ephesus*

You cannot dream yourself into character, you must hammer and forge yourself into one. ~ *Henry David Thoreau*

Your beliefs don't make you a better person, your behavior does. ~ *Unknown*

People do not seem to realize that their opinion of the world is also a confession of character. ~ *Ralph Waldo Emerson*

If you don't have enemies, you don't have character. ~ *Paul Newman*

Talent develops in quiet places, character develops in the full current of human life. ~ *Johann Wolfgang Von Goethe*

Greatness is not found in possessions, power, position or prestige. It is discovered in goodness, humility service and character. ~ *William Arthur Ward*

Coaching

A life coach does for the rest of your life, what a personal trainer does for your health and fitness. ~ *Elaine Macdonald*

We could all use a little coaching. When you're playing the game, it's hard to think of everything. ~ *Jim Rohn*

I know I wouldn't be here today if it weren't for working with mentors and coaches to break things down and help me discover my abilities and blind spots. ~ *Joshua Schneider*

Treat a person as he is and he will remain as he is. Treat him as he could be and he will become what he should be. ~ *Jimmy Johnson*

A coach's success is not measured in the number of wins he produced, but in the number of winners produced. ~ *Unknown*

Whoever admits that he is too busy to improve his methods has acknowledged himself to be at the end of his rope, and that is always the saddest predicament which anyone can get into. ~ *J. Ogden Armour*

Life has no limitations, except the ones you make. ~ *Les Brown*

One reason people resist change is that they focus on what they have to give up, rather than what they have to gain. ~ *Rick Godwin*

Never make yourself fell like nothing in order to make someone else fell like everything. ~ *Unknown*

The 18, 40, 60 rule: At 18 you worry about what everyone thinks of you. At 40 you don't care. At 60 you realize no one was thinking about you anyway! ~ *Daniel G. Amen, M.D.*

A coach is someone who tells you what you don't want to hear, who has you see what you don't want to see, so you can be who you have always known you could be. ~ *Tom Landry*

Investing in yourself is the best investment you will ever make. It will not only improve your life, it will improve the lives of those around you. ~ *Robin S. Sharma*

The difference between want and need is self-control. ~ *Unknown*

The pessimist sees difficulty in every opportunity. The optimist sees the opportunity in every difficulty. ~ *Winston Churchill*

Knowing others is intelligence; knowing yourself is true wisdom. Mastering others is strength; mastering yourself is true power. ~ *Lao Tzu*

Commitment

Commitment is that turning point in your life when you seize the moment and convert it into an opportunity to alter your destiny. ~ *Dennis Waitley*

Commitment means staying loyal to what you said you were going to do, long after the mood you said it in has left you. ~ *Unknown*

There's a difference between interest and commitment. When you're interested in doing something, you do it only when it's convenient. When you're "committed" to doing something, you accept no excuses, only results. ~ *Kenneth Blanchard*

Life's greatest rewards are reserved for those who demonstrate a never-ending commitment to act until they achieve. ~ *Anthony Robbins*

Think of an egg and realize, the pig was only involved, then imagine a slice of bacon and understand that the pig was committed. ~ *Daniel Gleed*

Once a man has made a commitment to a way of life, he puts the greatest strength in the world behind him. It's something we call heart power. Once a man has made his commitment, nothing will stop him short of success. ~ *Vince Lombardi*

Communication

How strangely we diminish something as soon as we try to express it in words. ~ *Maurice Maeterlinck*

Behind the need to communicate is the need to share. Behind the need to share is the need to be understood. ~ *Leo Rosten*

Talk to people about themselves and they will listen for hours. ~ *Benjamin Disraeli*

Euphemisms are unpleasant truths wearing diplomatic cologne.
~ *Quentin Crisp*

Speak when you are angry, and you will make the best speech you
will ever regret. ~ *Ambrose Bierce*

In a healthy relationship you should not be afraid to speak your
mind. No type of relationship should cause you to compromise
or doubt who you are. ~ *Talayah G. Stovall*

It's not what you tell them...it's what they hear. ~ *Red Auerbach*

The most important thing in communication is hearing what
isn't being said. ~ *Anonymous*

Keep your words soft and tender because tomorrow you may
have to eat them. ~ *Anonymous*

Never argue with a fool. Someone watching may not be able to
tell the difference. ~ *Anonymous*

When you're arguing with a fool, make sure he isn't doing the
same thing. ~ *Anonymous*

Kindness is a language the deaf can hear and the blind can see. ~
Anonymous

Never miss a good chance to shut up. ~ *Anonymous*

Effective communication is 20% what you know and 80% how
you feel about what you know. ~ *Jim Rohn*

Be sure to taste your words before you spit them out. ~ *Unknown*

The difference between the right word and the almost right word
is the difference between lightning and the lightning bug. ~ *Mark
Twain*

A single moment of misunderstanding is sometimes so
poisonous that it makes us forget within a minute the hundred
loveable moments spent together. ~ *Unknown*

Without a repeatable process of communication in place, our assumptions shape our relationships. They limit our vision and reduce the impact of our knowledge and experience. ~ *Garrison Wynn*

The single biggest problem in communication is the illusion that it has taken place. ~ *George Bernard Shaw*

Complaining

Complaining is finding faults, wisdom is finding solutions. ~ *Ajahn Brahm*

Comparing and complaining is the attitude of a person who doesn't have satisfaction in life. ~ *Unknown*

Spending today complaining about yesterday, won't make tomorrow any better. ~ *Unknown*

Realize that if you have time to whine and complain about something then you have the time to do something about it. ~ *Anthony J. D'angelo*

Complaining continues to create the vibration of what you don't want. Today, take your focus off what is wrong and focus on what is right and how you desire things to be. Put all your love, energy, mental power and –

decision making towards what you want and do not entertain thoughts that are to the contrary. ~ *Jackson Kiddard*

People who complain are like yellow traffic lights, nobody really pays any attention to them. ~ *Unknown*

Are you just complaining or are you proposing a solution? Anybody can complain, it takes creativity and guts to propose a solution. ~ *Dan O'donnell*

Compliment

When you first arrive at work, compliment someone, at lunch find another to compliment; before you go home at night be sure to pay a compliment to someone else. ~ *Fred Kyler*

I can run for a good 30 days on the strength of a compliment. ~ *Mark Twain*

A compliment is verbal sunshine ~ *Robert Orben*

One compliment from you is like a compliment from the world. ~ *Unknown*

An occasional compliment is necessary to keep up one's self-respect. ~ *Mark Twain*

If you look for something to criticize, you will find it. If you look for something to compliment you will find that too. Your choice. ~ *Katrina Mayer*

Confidence

The moment you start comparing yourself to others is the moment you lose confidence in yourself. ~ *Unknown*

Always act like you are wearing an invisible crown. ~ *Unknown*

Nobody can make you feel inferior without your consent. ~ *Eleanor Roosevelt*

It's not who you are that holds you back, it's who you think you're not. ~ *Unknown*

Confidence is the ability to feel beautiful without needing someone to tell you. ~ *Unknown*

The real beauty of a person comes from standing tall for what you believe in and showing confidence in yourself that you can make a difference. ~ *Unknown*

A tiger doesn't lose sleep over the opinion of sheep. ~ *Unknown*

Confidence is silent, insecurities are loud. ~ *Unknown*

Don't worry about those who talk behind your back. They're behind you for a reason. ~ *Unknown*

Courage

Courage doesn't mean you don't get afraid. Courage means you don't let fear stop you. ~ *Bethany Hamilton*

Courage is the first of human qualities because it is the quality which guarantees all others. ~ *Winston Churchill*

Courage doesn't happen when you have all the answers. It happens when you are ready to face the questions you have been avoiding your whole life. ~ *Shannon Alder*

He who is not courageous enough to take risks will accomplish nothing in life. ~ *Muhammad Ali*

Courage changes things for the better, with courage you can stay with something long enough to succeed at it, realizing that it usually takes two, three, or four times as long to succeed as you thought or hoped. ~ *Earl Nightingale*

To see what is right and not to do it is cowardice. ~ *Confucius*

With courage you will dare to take risks, have the strength to be compassionate and the wisdom to be humble. Courage is the foundation of integrity. ~ *Keshavan Nair*

Man cannot discover new oceans unless he has the courage to lose sight of the shore. ~ *Andre Gide*

Courage is not the absence of fear, it is moving forward in the presence of fear. ~ *Unknown*

He who loses wealth loses much, he who loses a friend loses more, but he who loses his courage loses all. ~ *Miguel De Cervantes*

Creativity

There is no doubt that creativity is the most important human resource of all. Without creativity, there would be no progress, and we would be forever repeating the same patterns. ~ *Edward de Bono*

Creativity is allowing yourself to make mistakes. Art is knowing which ones to keep. ~ *Scott Adams*

Creativity is thinking up new things. Innovation is doing new things. ~ *Theodore Levitt*

When we engage in what we are naturally suited to do, our work takes on the quality of play and it is play that stimulates creativity. ~ *Linda Naiman*

Creativity is just connecting things. When you ask creative people how they did something, they feel a little guilty because they didn't really do it, they were just able to connect experiences they've had and synthesize new things ~ *Steve Jobs*

Everything is made up of the exact same thing, whether it's your hand, the ocean, or a star. ~ *John Assaraf*

Passion is one great force that unleashes creativity because if your passionate about something your more willing to take risks. ~ *Unknown*

It is better to have enough ideas for some of them to be wrong, than to be always right by having no ideas at all. ~ *Edward de Bono*

Creativity is inventing, experimenting, growing, taking risks, breaking rules, making mistakes, and having fun. ~ *Mary Lou Cook*

The uncreative mind can spot wrong answers, but it takes a creative mind to spot wrong questions. ~ *Antony Jay*

Listen to anyone with an original idea, no matter how absurd it may sound at first. If you put fences around people, you get sheep. Give people the room they need. ~ *William McKnight*

Everyone who's ever taken a shower has had an idea. It's the person who gets out of the shower, dries off and does something about it who makes a difference. ~ *Nolan Bushnell*

All great deeds and all great thoughts have a ridiculous beginning. ~ *Albert Camus*

Ideas are like rabbits. You get a couple and learn how to handle them, and pretty soon you have a dozen. ~ *John Steinbeck*

If you hear a voice within you say, 'You cannot paint,' then by all means paint, and that voice will be silenced. ~ *Vincent van Gogh*

The world is but a canvas to the imagination. ~ *Henry David Thoreau*

Invention strictly speaking, is little more than a new combination of those images which have been previously gathered and deposited in the memory; nothing can come from nothing. ~ *Sir Joshua Reynolds*

You can't stop creativity, the more you use, the more you have. ~ *Maya Angelou*

It seems to be one of the paradoxes of creativity that in order to think originally, we must familiarize ourselves with the ideas of others. ~ *George Kneller*

We will discover the nature of our particular genius when we stop trying to conform to our own and other people's models and learn to be ourselves and allow our natural channel to open. ~ *Shakti Gawain*

No matter what you are currently able to do, creativity can make you capable of more. ~ *Unknown*

Daring ideas are like chessmen moved forward; they may be beaten, but they may start a winning game. ~ *Goethe*

To live a creative life, we must lose our fear of being wrong. ~ *Joseph Chilton Pierce Quotes*

One of my early mentors, poet David Wagoner, who divides the creative process into three phases – madman, poet and critic – once told me that you need to find your own magic to stay in the world of creative play. ~ *Sonia Gernes*

Do not fear to be eccentric in opinion, for every opinion now accepted was once eccentric. ~ *Bertrand Russell*

The difficulty lies not so much in developing new ideas as in escaping from old ones. ~ *John Maynard Keynes*

Critic

A critic is a man who knows the way but can't drive the car. ~ *David Ogilvy*

Concern over criticism clogs creativity. ~ *Duane Alan Hahn*

Before you criticize a man, walk a mile in his shoes. That way, when you do criticize him, you'll be a mile away and have his shoes. ~ *Steve Martin*

Great minds discuss ideas; average minds discuss events; small minds discuss people. ~ *Eleanor Roosevelt*

He who throws dirt always loses ground. ~ *Confucius*

A critic is a legless man who teaches running. ~ *Channing Pollock*

The pleasure we feel in criticizing robs us from being moved by very beautiful things. ~ *Jean De La Bruyere*

Criticism is the disapproval of people, not for having faults, but having faults different from your own. ~ *Unknown*

Any jackass can kick a barn down, but it takes a carpenter to build it. ~ *Sam Rayburn*

D

Decision

A real decision is measured by the fact that you've taken a new action. If there is no action, you haven't truly decided. ~ *Tony Robbins*

Your life changes the moment you make a new congruent committed decision. ~ *Anthony Robbins*

Don't base your decisions on the advice of people who don't have to deal with the result. ~ *Unknown*

No good decision was ever made in a swivel chair. ~ *George S. Patton*

Never make a decision when you're angry and never make a promise when you're happy. ~ *Unknown*

It is your decisions not your conditions, that determine your destiny. ~ Anthony Robbins.

I'm not a product of my circumstances, I am a product of my decisions. ~ *Stephen Covey*

I encourage you to consider and reconsider and then consider again before making permanent decisions based on temporary situations. The most expensive thing you can own is regret. ~ *Daniel Gleed*

Using the power of decision gives you the capacity to get past any excuse to change any and every part of your life in an instant. ~ *Tony Robbins*

Discipline

We all suffer one of two pains, the pain of discipline or the pain of regret. ~ *Joshua Schneider*

As human beings, we are responsible for our own lives. Our behavior is a function of our decisions, not our conditions. We can subordinate feelings to values. We have the initiative and the responsibility to make things happen. ~ *Stephen Covey*

Discipline is doing what you know needs to be done, even though you don't feel like doing it. ~ *Unknown*

Affirmation without discipline is the beginning of delusion. ~ *Jim Rohn*

Discipline is the bridge between goals and accomplishment. ~ *Anonymous*

Self-respect is the root of discipline; the sense of dignity grows with the ability to say no to one's self. ~ *Abraham Joshua Heschel*

Some people regard discipline as a chore. For me, it's a kind of order that sets me free to fly. ~ *Julie Andrews*

Life without discipline is like a ship without a rudder ~ *Harsh Metha*

Discipline is the virtue that begins in obedience and flowers in self-control. ~ *Ted Malloch*

Discipline is just choosing between what you want now and what you want the most. ~ *Anonymous*

Discipline is the refining fire by which talent becomes ability. ~ *Roy L. Smith*

Disappointment is the action of your brain readjusting itself to reality after discovering things are not the way you thought they were. ~ *Brad Warner*

Dreams

Show a man his future and he'll wait for it, show a man how to dream for his future and he'll create it. ~ *Joshua Schneider*

A dream is but a wish until it is written down. ~ *Unknown*

If one advances confidently in the direction of his dreams and endeavors to live the life which he has imagined, he will meet with a success unexpected in common hours. ~ *Henry David Thoreau*

The real power of having a dream is putting it into action. ~ *Talayah G. Stovall*

Dream lofty dreams, and as you dream, so shall you become. Your vision is the promise of what you shall one day be. Your ideal is the prophecy of what you shall at last unveil. ~ *James Lane Allen*

Dreams don't work unless you do. ~ *Unknown*

I cheated on my fears, broke up with my doubts, got engaged to my faith and now I'm marrying my dreams. ~ *Unknown*

E

Empower

One of the greatest gifts we can give other people is the empowerment to create a life they love, filled with purposeful, enjoyable work, and relationships they hold dear. ~ *Sarah L. Cook*

Often, it's the deepest pain which empowers you to grow into your highest self. ~ *Unknown*

Man was designed for accomplishment, engineered for success, and endowed with the seeds of greatness. ~ *Zig Ziglar*

You were put on this earth to achieve your greatest self, to live out your purpose and to do it fearlessly. ~ *Dr. Steve Maraboli*

The most common way people give up their power is by thinking they don't have any. ~ *Alice Walker*

No one can make you feel inferior without your consent. ~ *Eleanor Roosevelt*

I was told that if you work hard, bust your butt, go to school, and get great grades, you'd do well in life. That's a bunch of crap. Today we have better information about how the universe operates and how we operate. ~ *John Assaraf*

Your greatest self has been waiting your whole life, don't make it wait any longer. ~ *Dr. Steve Maraboli*

Everything you've ever desired to achieve here on earth already exists, the key is to live in high self-esteem and believe you are worthy of receiving it. ~ *Anonymous*

Whether you think you can or you can't. Your right! ~ *Henry Ford*

We simply can't control what comes out of other people mouths. However, we can control how we feel about what they say. ~ *Scarlett Jones*

The things that matter the most, must never be at the mercy of the things that matter the least. ~ *Goethe*

Next time you're in front of the mirror, let your heart be the one to observe, the mind can play tricks on you. Use the eyes of your heart to see what your mind cannot show. ~ *Unknown*

If you just set out to be liked, you would be prepared to compromise on anything at any time and you would achieve nothing. ~ *Margaret Thatcher*

When everything seems to be going against you, remember that an airplane takes off "against" the wind, not with it. ~ *Henry Ford*

Energy

Energy and persistence conquer all things. ~ *Benjamin Franklin*

Everything around is made up of energy. To attract positive things in life, start by giving off positive energy. ~ *Unknown*

When you are in harmony with yourself, everything unfolds with grace and ease. ~ *Panache Desai*

Miracles start to happen when we give as much energy to our dreams as we do to our fears. ~ *Richard Wilkins*

The level of energy you put out is the level of energy you attract. ~ *Rachel Bermingham*

Sin is energy in the wrong channel. ~ *Augustine*

The secret of change is to focus all of your energy, not on fighting the old, but building the new. ~ *Sacrates*

What are you tolerating that drains your energy? ~ *Unknown*

Enthusiasm

Enthusiasm is the mother of effort, nothing great was ever achieved without enthusiasm. ~ *Ralph Waldo Emerson*

Enthusiasm is that secret and harmonious spirit which hovers over the production of genius. ~ *Isaac D'israel*

Enthusiasm is a supernatural serenity. ~ *Henry David Thoreau*

Flaming enthusiasm, backed up by horse sense and persistence, is the quality that most frequently makes for success. ~ *Dale Carnegie*

Enthusiasm is the match that lights the candle of achievement. ~ *William Arthur Ward*

Success is the ability to go from failure to failure without losing your enthusiasm. ~ *Winston Churchill*

All we need to make us really happy is something to be enthusiastic about. ~ *Charles Kingsley*

You can do anything if you have enthusiasm. Enthusiasm is the yeast that makes your hopes rise to the stars. With it there is accomplishment, without it there are only alibis. ~ *Henry Ford*

You'll be surprised how powerful you can be when you infect others with your enthusiasm. ~ *Kitty Kolding*

A mediocre idea that generates enthusiasm will go further than a great idea that inspires no one. ~ *Mary Kay Ash*

The secret of genius is to carry the spirit of the child into old age, which means never losing your enthusiasm. ~ *Aldous Huxley*

Enthusiasm releases the drive to carry you over obstacles and adds significance to all you do. ~ *Norman Vincent Peale*

Specialized knowledge rightly applied is powerful, and enthusiasm flips the switch. ~ *Ivern Ball*

Executive Coaching

Globally executive coaching is increasingly being recognized both in the public and private sectors as one of the most effective ways to develop exceptional leaders. ~ *Gary Ranker*

It's helpful to start from what people are doing well, too often we start from what people need to change and what they're not doing so well. This deficit approach is often demotivating unless we begin from a more positive, optimistic stance. From there we can start to look at what the developmental issues are – and identify the next steps the person or team can take to make progress and improve performance. ~ *Peter Bluckert*

Coaching is assisting in the continual incremental release of a person's potential and helping them increase performance levels in themselves and their organization through discovering new things and uncovering what was already there, lying dormant beneath the surface. ~ *Daniel Gleed*

One of the key elements of successful coaching is awareness. My goal is to empower a person to become aware that there is a need for change and discover how the behaviors can be different. When the come upon the answers themselves, they are -

much more likely to have sense of ownership. ~ *Enrique Garcia Bajar*

Living with prolonged stress or stuck in unfinished business typically leaves us feeling exhausted, empty, anxious and depressed. Our perspective on life affects our decision-making and risk-taking and when our world-view shrinks, our desire lessens, and it impacts negatively on others. This underlines the importance of protecting our energy, and vitality. ~ *Peter Bluckert*

Your potential minus your limitations equals your performance, understand this and you are limitless. You have the hardware to move way beyond where you are and intuitively deep inside, you know this. Most performance problems are a result of your software, change the software, change your life. ~ *Ron and Kate Patulski*

You can only change what you are aware of, at the heart of all our work is the belief that awareness is ultimately the real change agent. Our job, and our core competence, is to facilitate a deeper level of awareness in the individuals and teams we work with. However, awareness does not automatically lead to change. Other factors come into play such as motivation to change, a vision of what may be possible, regular practice of new behaviors and a cultural context that supports change. ~ *Peter Bluckert*

Coaching is all about having someone believe in you and encourage you, it's about getting feedback, sparking new ideas, discovering blind spots. It's about looking at things from new perspectives and experiencing higher levels of personal and professional and spiritual growth. ~ *Daniel Gleed*

Exercise

Take care of your body, it's the only place you have to live in. ~ *Anonymous*

Fitness starts in your head. You must choose to eat clean, exercise regularly, and treat your body with respect. ~ *Susan Powter*

The Asian secret to healthy looking physic is to eat breakfast like a king, lunch like a queen and dinner like a pauper. ~ *Mary Angeline Gleed*

The only bad workout is the one that didn't happen. You choose. ~ *Anonymous*

I work out because I can. When I get tired or I'm short on time, or I want to quiet. I think about how lucky I am to be healthy enough to work out daily. Be grateful for your health and your ability to become stronger. Don't ever take that for granted. ~ *Unknown*

It's no coincidence that four of the six letters in health are "heal" ~ *Ed Northstrom*

Your life does not get better by chance, it gets better by change. ~ *Chuck Norris*

Exercise strengthens the body, relaxes the mind and toughens the spirit. ~ *Vinoba Bhave*

If you still look cute at the end of your workout, you didn't train hard enough. ~ *Unknown*

Every man is the builder of a temple called, his body. ~ *Henry David Thoreau*

If a man achieves victory over his body, who in the world can exercise power over him? He who rules himself rules over the whole world. ~ *Vinoba Bhave*

Go to the gym and become stronger than your strongest excuse. ~ *Gary Allen*

Excuses

Excuses are the nails used to build the house of failure. ~ *Anonymous*

Winners make goals, losers make excuses. ~ *Vince Lombardi*

Excuses are like male nipples. They're completely useless. ~ *Don Calame*

Humans make excuses to avoid blaming themselves. ~ *Natalia Lizardo*

Don't give up what you want most for what you want now. ~ *James Cash Penny*

He that is good for making excuses is seldom good for anything else. ~ *Benjamin Franklin*

Excuses are the words to fill the gap between wanting something and achieving something. ~ *Anonymous*

F

Failure

I missed more than 9000 shots in my career, I've lost almost 300 games. Twenty-six times I've been trusted to take the game winning shot and missed. I've failed over and over and over again in my life, and that is why I succeed. ~ *Michael Jordan*

I have not failed. I have just found 10,000 things that do not work. ~ *Thomas Edison (Invented the light bulb)*

I am not judged by the number of times I fail, but by the number of times I succeed. And the number of times I succeed is in direct proportion to the number of times I can fail and keep trying. ~ *Tom Hopkins.*

It's fine to celebrate your success but it is more important to heed the lessons of failure. ~ *Bill gates*

A failure is not always a mistake, it may simply be the best one can do under the circumstances. The real mistake is to stop trying. ~ *B.F. Skinner*

There is no such thing as failure, only varying degrees of strength. ~ *Daniel Gleed*

Ninety nine percent of all failures come from people who have a habit of making excuses. ~ *George Washington Carver*

Faith

Faith does not make things easy, it makes them possible. ~ *Luke*

Faith is taking the first step even though you don't see the whole staircase. ~ *Martin Luther King Jr.*

Your future is as bright as your faith. ~ *Thomas Monson*

Faith is to believe what we do not see. The reward of faith is to see what we believe. ~ *Saint Augustine*

I do not have to be directed by anything outside of myself. God is within me, and the infinite and divine power that gives me sustenance as a human being is always there. ~ *Wayne Dyer*

Not everything that is faced can be changed. But nothing can be changed until it is faced. ~ *James Baldwin*

Faith is the first factor in a life devoted to service. Without it nothing is possible. With it nothing is impossible. ~ *Mary Mcleod Bethune*

Faith is the substance of things hoped for and the evidence of things not seen. ~ *Hebrews*

Faith is a knowledge within the heart, beyond the reach of proof. ~ *Kahlil Gibran*

Fear

Do the thing you fear the most and it will soon become your ally. ~ *Unknown*

If you live in fear of the future because of what happened in your past, you'll end up losing what you have in the present. ~ *Anonymous*

Nothing in life is to be feared, it is to be understood. ~ Marie Curie

Fear is the main source of superstition, and one of the main sources of cruelty, to conquer fear is the beginning of wisdom. ~ *Bertrand Russell*

Too many of us are not living our dreams because we are living our fears. ~ *Les Brown*

Miracles start when you give as much energy to your dreams as you do to your fears. ~ *Richard Wilkins*

Do the thing you fear, and the death of fear is certain. ~ *Ralph Waldo* Emerson

Fear defeats more people than any one thing in the world. ~ *Ralph Waldo* Emerson

I cheated on my fears, broke up with my doubts, got engaged to my faith, and now I'm married to my dreams. ~ Unknown

Too many of us are not living our dreams because we are busy living our fears. ~ *Les Brown*

Flexibility

The stiffest tree is most easily cracked while bamboo or willow survives by bending with the wind. ~ *Bruce Lee*

Strong character should be combined with flexibility of the mind. ~ *Unknown*

Those who are flexible in thought will inevitably succeed. ~ *David Cunliffe*

Flexibility is a requirement for survival. ~ *Roger Von Oech*

Intelligence is the handmaiden of flexibility and change. ~ *Vernor Vinge*

Focus

One recognizes one's course by discovering the paths that stray away from it. ~ *Albert Camus*

People think focus means saying yes to the thing you've got to focus on. But that's not what it means at all. It means saying no to the hundred other good ideas that there are. You have to pick carefully. ~ *Steve Jobs*

The successful warrior is the average man with laser like focus. ~ *Bruce Lee*

Let go of things you can't change and focus on the things you can. You can't depend on your eyes when your imagination is out of focus. ~ *Napoleon Hill*

Concentrate all your thoughts on the work at hand. The sun's rays do not burn until brought into focus. ~

Alexander Grahm Bell

If you focus on results you will never change. If you focus on change, you will get results. ~ *Jack Dixion*

The secret of change is to focus all your energy, not on fighting the old but building the new. ~ *Socrates*

You can either focus on whats tearing you apart of what's holding you together. ~ *Alan Alda*

Change your focus from making money to serving more people. Serving more people makes the money come in. ~ *Robert Kyosaki*

Forgiveness

For me, forgiveness and compassion are always linked; how do we hold people accountable for wrong doing and yet at the same time remain in touch with their humanity enough to believe in their capacity to be transformed. ~ *Bell Hooks*

Forgive others not only because they deserve forgiveness, whether you feel they deserve it or not, but most importantly because you deserve peace. ~ Dr. *James Dobson*

We achieve inner health only through forgiveness, the forgiveness not only of others and also of ourselves. ~ *Joshua Loth Liebman*

Forgiveness does not change the past, but it does enlarge the future. ~ *Jim Rohn*

Lack of forgiveness causes almost all of our self-sabotaging behavior. ~ *Mark Victor Hansen*

Forgiveness is unlocking the door to set someone free and realize that you were a prisoner. ~ *Max Lucado*

You will know that forgiveness has begun when you recall those who have hurt you and feel the power to wish them well. ~ Lewis B. Smedes

Forgiveness is having given up all hope of having a bitter past. ~ *Anne Lamott*

The weak can never forgive, forgiveness is the attribute of the strong. ~ *Gandhi*

He who cannot forgive others breaks the bridge over which he himself must pass. ~ *Confucius*

Without forgiveness life is governed by an endless cycle of resentment and retaliation. ~ *Roberto Assagioli*

Forgiveness is a gift you give yourself. ~ *Tony Robbins*

To forgive is the highest, most beautiful form of love, in return you will receive untold peace and happiness. ~ *Robert Muller*

Never forget three of the most powerful resources you have available to you. Love, prayer and forgiveness. ~ *H. Jackson Brown Jr*

Freedom

Socialists, can provide you shelter, fill your belly with bacon and beans, treat you when your ill, and all the things guaranteed to a prisoner or a slave. ~ *Ronald Reagan*

Freedom is the oxygen of the soul. ~ *Moshe Dayan*

The only way to deal with an UN-free world is to become so absolutely free that your very existence is an act of rebellion. ~ *Albert Camus*

Nobody can give you freedom, nobody can give you equality or justice. If you are a man, "you take it." ~ *Malcom X*

Caged birds accept each other but flight is what they long for. ~ *Tennessee Williams.*

If the freedom of speech is taken away, then dumb and silent we may be led, like sheep to the slaughter. ~ *George Washington*

I prefer dangerous freedom over peaceful slavery. ~ *Thomas Jefferson*

Conformity is the jailer of freedom and the enemy of growth. ~ *John F. Kennedy*

Freedom is never more than one generation away from extinction. We didn't pass it to our children in the bloodstream. It must be fought for, protected, and handed on for them to do the same, or one day we'll spend our sunset years telling our children and our children's children what it was once like in the United States where men were free. ~ *Ronald Reagan*

I am a free spirit, either admire me from the ground or fly with me. But don't ever try to cage me. ~ *Anonymous*

Freedom is not defined by safety. Freedom is defined by the ability of citizens to live without government interference. Government cannot create a world without risks, nor would we really with to live in such a fictional place. ~ *Ron Paul*

Frequency

Everything is energy and that is all there is to it. Match the frequency of the reality you want, and you cannot help but get that reality. There can be no other way, this is not philosophy, this is physics. ~ *Albert Einstein*

Whatever you think about activates a vibration within you. ~ *Abraham Hicks*

Alpha waves in the human brain are between 6 and 8 hertz. The wave frequency of the human cavity resonates between 6 and 8 hertz. All biological systems operate in the same frequency range. The human brains alpha waves function in this range and the electrical resonance of the earth is between 6 and 8 hertz. Thus, our entire biological system, the brain and the earth itself, work on the same frequencies. If we can control that resonate system electronically, we can directly control the entire mental system of humankind ~ *Nicola Tesla*

The scale of light can be described by numbers, called the frequency, and as the numbers get higher, the light goes from red to blue to ultraviolet. We can't see ultraviolet light, but it can affect photographic plates. It's still light. ~ *Richard Feynman*

Everything changes when you start to emit your own frequency rather than absorbing the frequencies around you. When you start imprinting your intent on the universe rather than receiving an imprint from existence. ~ *Barbara Marciniak*

The entire human psyche is part of the entire universal electromagnetic field and it is nurtured by that frequency and that touch. ~ *Harbhajan Singh Yogi*

The most fascinating revelation is that humanity can tune into a consistently higher frequency through the power of peace and inner stillness. ~*Christopher Dines*

The universe sends out the highest vibrations of love to you and your transmitter, your open heart resonates with this frequency. ~ *Tonja Christine Faeger*

In the matter of friends, align yourself with those who vibrate at the energy level and frequency you wish to be at. ~ *William Constantine*

For your mind, emotions and physical body to be working together in total harmony, the chakras need to be spinning at the correct frequency. ~ *Stephen Richards*

Let others vibrate as they vibrate and want the best for them. Never mind how they're flowing to you. You concentrate on how you're flowing. Because one who is connected to the energy stream is more powerful, more influential than a million who are not. ~ *Abraham*

Friendship

Friendship improves happiness and abates misery, by the doubling of our joy and the dividing of our grief. ~ *Marcus Tullius Cecero*

Good friends are like stars, you don't always see them, but you know they're always there. ~ *Unknown*

Friendship is a strong and habitual inclination in two persons to promote the good and happiness of one another. ~ *Eustace Budgell*

Best friends are people you know that you don't need to talk to every day. You don't even need to talk to each other for weeks, but when you do, it's like you never stopped talking. ~ *Anonymous*

True friends stab you in the *front*. ~ *Oscar Wilde*

In the rhythm of life, we sometimes find ourselves out of tune, but as long as there are friends to provide the melody, the music plays on. ~ *Elvis Presley*

A friend is someone who walks in when others walk out. ~ *Walter Winchell*

Friendship isn't one big thing, it's a million little things. ~ *Ryann*

It's better to cry than be angry, because anger hurts others while tears flow silently through the soul and cleanse the heart. ~ *Pope John Paul The 2nd*

A true friend is one who thinks you're a good egg, even if you're half cracked. ~ *Unknown*

G

Giving

The law of giving is very simple, if you want joy, give joy. If you seek love, offer love. If you crave material affluence, help others become prosperous. ~ *Deepak Chopra*

We make a living by what we get, and we make a life by what we give. ~ *Winston Churchill*

No one can control their destiny unless they give "to" themselves as much as they give "of" themselves. ~ *Suze Orman*

Any kind gesture can reach a wound that only compassion can heal. ~ *Steve Maraboli*

What we do for ourselves dies with us, what we do for others and the world remains and is immortal. ~ *Albert Pine*

The best way to cheer yourself up is to cheer someone else up. ~ *Kahlil Gibran*

Generosity is the habit of giving freely without expecting anything in return. ~ *Unknown*

Great opportunities to help others seldom come, but small ones surround us every day. ~ *Sally Koch*

Real generosity is doing something nice for someone who will never find out. ~ *Frank A. Clark*

Attention is the rarest and purest form of generosity. ~ *Simone Well*

There is overwhelming evidence that the higher the level of self-esteem, the more likely one will be to treat others with respect, kindness and generosity. ~ *Nathaniel Branden*

Be happy with what you have and are. Be generous with both, and you won't have to hunt for happiness. ~ *William E. Gladstone*

We can't help everyone, but everyone can help someone. ~ *Dr. Loretta Scott*

There are those that give with joy and that joy is their reward. ~ *Kahlil Gibran*

The meaning of life is to find your gift, the purpose of life is to give it away. ~ *Pablo Picasso*

It's not how much we give but how much love we put into giving. ~ *Mother Teresa*

The best way to find yourself is to lose yourself in the service of others. ~ *Mahatma Gandhi*

To give away money is an easy matter in any man's power. But to decide to whom to give it, and how large and when, and for what purpose and how, is neither in every man's power nor an easy matter. ~ *Aristotle*

The manner of giving is worth more than the gift. ~ *Pierre Corneille*

I have found that among its other benefits, giving liberates the soul of the giver ~ *Maya Angelou*

Goals

A goal properly set is halfway reached. ~ *Abraham Lincoln*

A dream is just a dream, a goal is a dream with a plan and a deadline. ~ *Harvey Mackay*

Discipline is the bridge between goals and accomplishment. ~ *Jim Rohn*

Anyone who has ever ridden a bicycle knows that in order to move forward, you have to keep pedaling. Once you stop moving, you will fall off the bike. The same is true with your goals. Once we stop taking action, we lose our forward momentum and our goals will fall off. ~ *Talayah G. Stovall*

Big goals get big results. No goals get no results or somebody else's results. ~ *Mark Victor Hansen*

If you set goals and go after them with all the determination you can muster, your gifts will take you places that will amaze you. ~ *Les Brown*

Set a goal to achieve something that is so big, so exhilarating that it excites you and scares you at the same time. ~ *Bob Proctor*

Chunk down your goals with the right strategies and action steps and ensure that they are aligned to enable maximum achievement. ~ *Jack Canfield and Angelina Cheong*

If people are not laughing at your goals, your goals are too small. ~ *Unknown*

Setting goals is the first step in turning the invisible into the visible. ~ *Tony Robbins*

Gratitude

Gratitude opens the portals to a richer more abundant life. ~ *Unknown*

It is not happy people who are thankful, it is thankful people who are happy. ~ *Unknown*

Thankfulness is the beginning of gratitude. Gratitude is the completion of thankfulness. Thankfulness may consist merely of words. Gratitude is shown in acts. ~ *Henri Frederic*

Gratitude for the seemingly insignificant is the seed that plants a giant miracle ~ *Ann Voskamp*

Gratitude unlocks the usefulness of life: it turns what we have into enough and more, it turns denial into acceptance, chaos to order, confusion to clarity, it can turn a meal into a feast, a house into a home, a stranger into a friend. Gratitude makes sense of our past, brings peace for today and creates a vision for tomorrow. ~ *Melody Beattie*

Every day is a gift because it can either be the first day of the rest of our life or be our last day here on earth. ~ *Jim Stovall*

Gratitude is an attitude that hooks us up to our source of supply. And the more grateful you are, the closer you become to your maker, to the architect of the universe, to the spiritual core of your being. It's a phenomenal lesson. ~ Bob Proctor

He is a wise man who does not grieve for the things which he has not but rejoices for those which he has." ~ *Epictetus*

Gratitude opens the door to the power, the wisdom and the creativity of the universe. ~ *Deepak Chopra*

Let's start with what we can be thankful for, and get our mind into that vibration, and then watch the good that starts to come, because one thought leads to another thought. ~ *Bob Proctor*

We think we have to do something to be grateful, or something has to be done in order for us to be grateful, when gratitude is a state of being. ~ *Iyalna Vanzant*

Gratitude is the single most important ingredient to living a successful and fulfilled life. ~ *Jack Canfield*

The secret of abundance is to stop focusing on what you do not have and shift your consciousness to an appreciation for all that you are and all that you do have. ~ *Wayne Dyer*

In those times when we yearn to have more in our lives, we should dwell on the things we already have. In doing so, we will often find that our lives are already full to overflowing. ~ *Jim Stovall (Author of "The Ultimate Gift")*

Let gratitude be the pillow on which you kneel to say your nightly prayer. ~ *Maya Angelou*

When you practice gratefulness, there is a sense of respect towards others. ~ *The Dalai Lama*

H

Habits

Feeling sorry for yourself in your present condition, is not only a waste of energy but the worst habit you could possibly have. ~ *Dale Carnegie*

We are what we repeatedly do. Excellence then, is not an act, but a habit. ~ *Aristotle*

Keep your conscious mind busy with the expectation of the best, and your subconscious will faithfully reproduce your habitual thinking. ~ *Joseph Murphy*

Your thoughts become words, your words become actions, your actions become habits, habits shape character and character determines your destiny. ~ *James Allen*

Good habits once established are just as hard to break as bad habits. ~ *Robert Puller*

We first make our habits and then our habits make us. ~ *Napoleon Hill*

You cannot change your future, but you can change your habits, and surely your habits will change your future. ~ *Dr. Abdul Kalam*

Chains of habit are too light to be felt until they are too heavy to be broken. ~ *Warren Buffett*

Happiness

Happiness is like a kiss. You must share it to enjoy it. ~ *Bernard Meltzer*

For every minute of anger, you lose 60 seconds of happiness. ~ *Stephen Covey*

Everyone wants happiness, no one wants pain. But you can't make a rainbow, without a little rain. ~ *Og Mandina*

Sometimes the things you are most afraid of are the things that make you the happiest. ~ *Napoleon Hill*

Happiness is when what you think, what you say and what you do are in harmony. ~ *Gandhi*

If you want to live a happy life, tie it to a goal and not to people or things. ~ *Albert Einstein*

As human beings we all want to be happy and free from misery. We have learned that the key to happiness is inner peace. The greatest obstacles to inner peace are disturbing emotions such as anger, attachment, fear and suspicion, while love and compassion and a sense of universal responsibility are the sources of peace and happiness. ~ *Dalai Lama*

Happiness is like a butterfly, the more you chase it the more it eludes you. But if you turn your attention to other things, it comes and sits softly on your shoulder. ~ *Henry David Thoreau*

Happiness is not determined by what's happening around you, but rather what's happening inside you. ~ *Unknown*

Health

It's no coincidence that four of the six letters in health are "heal" ~ *Ed Northstrum*

Take care of your body, it's the only place you have to live. ~ *Jim Rohn*

The biggest issue by far is that carbohydrates are absolutely at the cornerstone of all of our major degenerative conditions. ~ *David Perlmutter*

Not taking care of your body is like not paying the rent, you end up with no place to live. ~ *Dr. Gayle Olinekova*

Caffeine restricts blood flow to the brain. And it also dehydrates the brain and the body. ~ *Daniel G. Amen, M.D.*

Every time you eat or drink you are either feeding disease or fighting it. ~ *Heather Morgan*

The food we eat goes beyond its macronutrients of carbohydrates, fat and protein. It's information. It interacts with and instructs our genome with every mouthful, changing genetic expression. ~ *David Perlmutter*

You can interfere with the normal rhythm of your heart, lungs, and other organs by worry, anxiety and fear. Feed your subconscious with thoughts of harmony, health and peace and all the functions of your body will become normal again. ~ *Joseph Murphy*

People who laugh actually live longer than people who don't. Few people realize that health actually varies according to the amount of laughter. ~ *James J. Walsh*

No diet will remove all the fat from your body because the brain is entirely fat. Without a brain, you might look good, but all you could do is run for public office. ~ George Bernard Shaw

If you keep good food in your fridge, you will eat good food. ~ *Errick Mcadams*

Those who think they have no time for healthy eating, will sooner or later have to find time for illness. ~ *Unknown*

I have chosen to be happy because it's good for my health. ~ *Voltaire*

Dried oregano has thirty times the brain-healing antioxidant power of raw blueberries, forty-six times more than apples, and fifty-six times as much as strawberries, making it one of the most powerful brain cell protectors on the planet. ~ *Daniel G. Amen, M.D.*

The food you eat can be either the safest and most powerful form of medicine or the slowest form of poison. ~ *Ann Wigmore*

Shoot for a total of no more than 80 grams of carbs in your daily diet. This means favoring vegetables that grow above ground like kale, broccoli, spinach, and cauliflower as opposed to those that store carbohydrate in the form of starch like potatoes and beets. ~ *David Perlmutter*

To ensure good health, eat lightly, breathe deeply, live moderately, cultivate cheerfulness, and maintain an interest in life. ~ *William Londen*

The Number of Hours You Sleep Each Night: One of the fastest ways to hurt your brain is to get fewer than seven or eight hours of sleep at night. People who typically get six hours or fewer of sleep have lower overall blood flow to the brain, which hurts its function. ~ *Daniel G. Amen*

Your attitude and your choices equal your life. ~ *Jim Rohn*

Let your food be your medicine and your medicine be your food. ~ *Hippocrates*

The ground work of all happiness is good health. ~ *Leigh Hunt*

Most people throughout the world, not just in Newport Beach, care more about their faces, their boobs, their bellies, their butts, and their abs than they do their brains. But it is your brain that is the key to having the face, the breasts, the belly, the butt, the abs, and the overall health you have always wanted; and it is brain dysfunction, in large part, that ruins our bodies and causes premature aging. ~ *Daniel G. Amen, M.D.*

Hope

The natural flights of the human mind are not from pleasure to pleasure, but from hope to hope. ~ *Samuel Johnson*

Sometimes good things fall apart so better things can fall together. ~ *Marilyn Monroe*

Hope is not dead, it is just larger than our imaginations; its purpose extending far beyond our comprehension. ~ *Kathy Hobaugh*

Hope is the feeling you get that the feeling have isn't permanent. ~ Jeann Kerr

Hope is faith holding out its hand in the dark. ~ *George Iles*

Hope is the companion of power and the mother of success, for who so hopes strongly has within him the gift of miracles. ~ *Og Mandino*

When you say that a situation or a person is hopeless, you are slamming the door in the face of god. ~ *Max Lucado*

Hope is the only bee that makes honey without flowers. ~ *Robert G. Ingersoll*

Hope is like the sun, which, as we journey toward it, casts the shadow of our burden behind us. ~ *Samuel Smiles*

Hugs

Millions and millions of years would still not give me half enough time to describe that tiny instant of eternity when you put your arms around me and I put my arms around you. ~ *Jacques Prevert*

A hug is two hearts wrapped in arms. ~ *Unknown*

Everybody needs a hug. It changes your metabolism. ~ *Leo Buscaglia*

A silent hug means a thousand words to an unhappy heart. ~ *Unknown*

Hugging closes the door to hate. ~ *Tony Davis*

Hugs, hand-shakes, even a good intentioned touch, transfers useful energy to boost the immune mechanism in the body. ~ *Unknown*

If for every tear I get a hug from you, then I would cry forever. ~ *Unknown*

Hugs don't need new equipment, special batteries or parts - just open up your arms and open up your hearts. ~ *Jill Wolf*

I have a present for you, but I need to borrow your arms for wrapping paper. ~ *Unknown*

Humility

Pride is concerned with "who" is right. Humility is concerned with "what" is right. ~ *Ezra T. Benson*

Humility is the mother of giants. One sees great things from the valley, only small things from the peak. ~ *G.K. Chesterton*

Humility is not thinking less of yourself but thinking of yourself less. ~ *C.S. Lewis*

Being humble means recognizing that we are not on earth to see how important we can become, but to see how much difference we can make in the lives of others. ~ *Gordon B. Hinkley*

There is nothing noble in being superior to your fellow man. True nobility is being superior to your former self. ~ *Ernest Hemingway*

The higher we are placed, the more humble we should walk. ~ *Dennis Waitley*

The humble person makes room for progress, the proud person believes they are already there. ~ *Ed Parker*

True humility is strength, not weakness. It disarms antagonism and ultimately conquers it. ~ *Meher Baba*

True humility is intelligent self-respect which keeps us from thinking too highly or too meanly of ourselves. It makes us modest by reminding us of how far we have come short of what we can be. ~ *Ralph W. Sockman*

Ego kills knowledge, as knowledge requires learning, and learning requires humility. ~ *Rolsey*

Beginning of all knowledge comes from humility. ~ *Jim Rohn*

Humility leads to strength and not to weakness. It is the highest form of self-respect to admit mistakes and to make amends for them. ~ *John J. Mcloy*

Only humility will help us grow. The feeling of I and mine obstructs the possibility of inner growth. ~ *Amma*

Humility is the ability to give up your pride and still retain your dignity. ~ *Vanna Bonta*

The x-factor of great leadership is not personality it is humility. ~ *Jim Collins*

Pride makes us artificial, humility makes us real. ~ *Thomas Merton*

It was pride that changed angels into devils. It is humility that makes men as angels. ~ *St. Augustine*

Humorous Quotes

If you think you are too small to be effective, you have never been in the dark with a mosquito. ~ *Betty Reese*

Friends are like knickers. Some crawl up your ass, some snap under pressure, some don't have the strength to hold you up, some get a little twisted, some are your favorite, some you can see right thru, some are cheap and just plain nasty, and some actually cover your ass when you need them to. Some you just hang out to dry. ~ *Unknown*

If you think nobody cares if you're alive, try missing a couple of car payments. ~ *Flip Wilson*

I have six locks on my door all in a row. When I go out, I lock every other one. I figure no matter how long somebody stands there picking the locks, they are always locking three. ~ *Elayne Boosler*

How is it that one careless match can start a forest fire, but it takes a whole box to start a campfire? ~ *Unknown*

A diplomat is someone who can tell you to go to hell in such a way that you will look forward to the trip. ~ *Caskie Stinnett*

Children: You spend the first 2 years of their life teaching them to walk and talk. Then you spend the next 16 telling them to sit down and shut-up. ~ *Unknown*

I couldn't repair your brakes, so I made your horn louder. ~ *Steven Wright*

A stockbroker urged me to buy a stock that would triple its value every year. I told him, at my age, I don't even buy green bananas. ~ *Claude Pepper*

Friendship is like peeing on yourself: everyone can see it, but only you get the warm feeling that it brings. ~ *Robert Bloch*

My therapist told me the way to achieve true inner peace is to finish what I start. So far, I've finished two bags of M&Ms and a chocolate cake. I feel better already. ~ *Dave Barry*

If at first you don't succeed, skydiving is not for you. ~ *Unknown*

To err is human, to blame it on somebody else shows management potential. ~ *Anonymous*

When you go into court you are putting your fate into the hands of twelve people who weren't smart enough to get out of jury duty. ~ *Norm Crosby*

Give a man a fish and he will eat for a day. Teach him how to fish, and he will sit in a boat and drink beer all day. ~ *Unknown*

A bargain is something you don't need at a price you can't resist. ~ *Franklin Jones*

Why do people say "no offense" right before they're about to offend you? ~ *Unknown*

By all means, marry. If you get a good wife, you'll become happy; if you get a bad one, you'll become a philosopher. ~ *Socrates*

I asked God for a bike, but I know God doesn't work that way. So, I stole a bike and asked for forgiveness. ~ *Emo Philips*

Never, under any circumstances, take a sleeping pill and a laxative on the same night. ~ *Dave Barry*

Get well cards have become so humorous that if you don't get sick you're missing half the fun. ~ *Flip Wilson*

I don't have a girlfriend. But I do know a woman who'd be mad at me for saying that. ~ *Mitch Hedberg*

Experience is something you don't get until just after you need it. ~ *Unknown*

Before I got married I had six theories about bringing up children; now I have six children and no theories. ~ *John Wilmot*

Two things are infinite: the universe and human stupidity; and I'm not sure about the universe. ~ *Albert Einstein*

I prefer to be a pessimist; it makes it easier to deal with my inevitable failure. ~ *Film: The McMullen Brothers*

My choices in life were either to be a piano player in a whore house or a politician. And to tell the truth, there's hardly any difference! ~ *Harry Truman*

My favorite machine at the gym is the vending machine. ~ Caroline Rhea

I always arrive late at the office, but I make up for it by leaving early. ~ *Charles Lamb*

A filing cabinet is a place where you can lose things systematically. ~ *T.H. Thompson*

If you even dream of beating me you'd better wake up and apologize. ~ *Muhammad Ali*

Inside me there's a thin person struggling to get out, but I can usually sedate him with four or five cupcakes. ~ *Bob Thaves*

To attract men, I wear a perfume called New Car Interior. ~ *Rita Rudner*

At every party, there are two kinds of people–those who want to go home and those who don't. The trouble is, they are usually married to each other. ~ *Ann Landers*

Politicians and diapers have one thing in common. They should both be changed regularly, and for the same reason. ~ *Jose Maria De Eca De Queiroz*

Life expectancy would grow by leaps and bounds if green vegetables smelled as good as bacon. ~ *Doug Larson*

Tell a man there are 300 billion stars in the universe and he'll believe you. Tell him a bench has wet paint on it and he'll have to touch it to be sure. ~ *Probably a Woman*

The human brain is a wonderful thing. It starts working the moment you are born, and never stops until you stand up to speak in public. ~ *George Jessel*

It is amazing how quickly the kids learn to drive a car, yet are unable to understand the lawn mower, snowblower and vacuum cleaner. ~ *Ben Bergor*

An archaeologist is the best husband a woman can have; the older she gets the more interested he is in her. ~ *Agatha Christie*

We are all here on earth to help others; what on earth the others are here for I don't know. ~ *W. H. Auden*

Put your hand on a hot stove for a minute, and it seems like an hour. Sit with a pretty girl for an hour, and it seems like a minute. That's relativity. ~ *Albert Einstein*

My grandmother started walking five miles a day when she was sixty. She's ninety-seven now, and we don't know where the hell she is. ~ *Unknown*

Do not take life too seriously. You will never get out of it alive. ~ *Elbert Hubbard*

To avoid criticism, do nothing, say nothing, and be nothing. ~ *Elbert Hubbard*

If you talk to God, you are praying; if God talks to you, you have schizophrenia. ~ *Thomas Szasz*

I'm sick of following my dreams. I'm just going to ask them where they're goin', and hook up with them later. ~ M*itch Hedberg*

Life is a sexually transmitted terminal illness, you're born knowing that you will die. Being fully aware that your days are numbered seems like a key motivator to live life to the fullest. ~ *Daniel Gleed*

I

Ideas

An idea can turn to dust or magic, depending on the talent that rubs against it. ~ *Bill Bernbach*

If you can't write your idea on the back of my business card, you don't have a clear idea. ~ *David Balasco*

Ideas have a short shelf life. You must act on them before the expiration date. ~ *Anonymous*

Ideas not coupled with action never become bigger than the brain cells they occupied. ~ *Arnold Glasow*

It's not how many ideas you have, it's how many ideas you make happen. ~ *David Ogilvy*

A persons mind once stretched by a new idea, never returns to its original dimensions. ~ *Unknown*

Ideas attract money, time, talents, skills, energy and other complementary ideas that will bring them into reality. ~ *Mark Victor Hansen*

Great minds discuss ideas. Average minds discuss events, and small minds discuss people. ~ *Eleanor Roosevelt*

The best way to have a good idea is to have lots of ideas. ~ *Linus Pauling*

Be less curious about people and more curious about ideas. ~ *Marie Curie*

Ideas are themselves substantive entities with the power to influence and even transform human life. Ideas are not unlike food, vitamins or vaccines. They invoke human potential for growth and development and can affect the course of evolution. ~ *Dr. Jonas Salk*

Imagination

The man who has no imagination, has no wings. ~ *Muhammad Ali*

Imagination is more important than knowledge, for knowledge is limited to all we now know and understand. Imagination embraces the entire world, and all there ever will be to know and understand. ~ *Albert Einstein*

You can't depend on your eyes if your imagination is out of focus. ~ *Mark Twain*

Limitations live only in our minds. But if we use our imaginations, our possibilities become endless. ~ *James Allen*

Logic will take you from A to B, imagination will take you everywhere. ~ *Albert Einstein*

Imagination is everything, imagination is our preview to life's coming attractions. ~ *Albert Einstein*

Every child is born blessed with a vivid imagination. But just as a muscle grows flabby with disuse, so the bright imagination of a child pales in later years if he fails to exercise it. ~ *Walt Disney*

The greatest gift ever given to you is your imagination, within it is the capacity to have all your wishes fulfilled. Look around you, everything that you can experience with your senses was once in someone's imagination. ~ *Dennis Waitley*

Impossible

Impossible is just a big word thrown around by small men who find it easier to live in the world they've been given than to explore the power they have to change it. Impossible is not a fact. It's an opinion. Impossible is not a declaration, it's a dare. Impossible is potential, impossible is temporary, impossible is nothing. ~ *Muhammad Ali*

Impossible only means that you haven't found the solution yet. ~ *Voltaire*

The person who says something is impossible, should not interrupt the person who is doing it. ~ *Chinese Proverb*

Impossible is a word only to be found in a dictionary of fools. ~ *Napoleon Bonaparte*

Only he that can see the invisible can do the impossible. ~ *Frank Gaines*

Innovation

You can't just ask customers what they want and then try to give that to them. By the time you get it built, they'll want something new. ~ *Steve Jobs*

I am looking for a lot of people who have an infinite capacity to not know what can't be done. ~ *Henry Ford*

Meaningful innovation does not need to be based on outright invention. Rather, there is an exhilarating shortcut. It is based on bold, new combinations of already existing components that simultaneously unlock height – ened levels of consumer value and reduce costs. ~ *Gabor George Burt*

When it comes to innovation, an ounce of execution is worth more than a ton of theory. ~ *Phil Mckinney*

Intuition will tell the thinking mind where to look next. ~ *Jonas Salk*

The dirty little secret—the fact often denied—is that unlike the mythical epiphany, real creation is sloppy. Discovery is messy; exploration is dangerous. No one knows what he's going to get when he's being creative. Filmmakers, painters, inventors, and entrepreneurs describe their work as a search: they explore the unknown hoping to find new things worth bringing to the world. And just like with other kinds of explorers, their search for ideas demands risk: much of what's found won't be satisfactory. Therefore, creative work cannot fit neatly into plans, budgets, and schedules. ~ *Scott Berkun*

Do not fear mistakes. There are none. ~ *Miles Davis*

There is only one thing stronger than all the armies of the world: and that is an idea whose time has come. ~ *Victor Hugo*

If you lose the power to laugh, you lose the power to think. ~ *Clarence Darrow*

When a good idea comes, part of my job is to move it around, just see what different people think, get people talking about it, argue with people about it, get ideas moving...get different people together to explore different aspects of it quietly, and, you know – just explore things. ~ *Steve Jobs*

Creativity is just connecting things. When you ask creative people how they did something, they feel like a little guilty because they didn't really do it, they just saw something. It seemed obvious to them after a while. That's because they were able to connect experiences they've had and synthesize new things. And the reason they were able to do that was that - they've had more experiences, or they have thought more about their experiences than other people. ~ *Steve Jobs*

Ideas are like rabbits. You get a couple and learn how to handle them, and pretty soon you have a dozen. ~ *John Steinbeck*

It is the essence of genius to make use of the simplest ideas. ~ *Charles Peguy*

There's no good idea that cannot be improved on. ~ *Michael Eisner*

We don't see things as they are, we see things as we are. ~ *Anais Nin*

Give me the young man who has brains enough to make a fool of himself. ~ *Robert Louis Stevenson*

Whatever you can do, or dream you can, begin it. Boldness has genius, power and magic in it. ~ *Goethe*

The greater the contrast, the greater the potential. Great energy only comes from a correspondingly great tension of opposites. ~ *Carl Jung*

99 percent of success is built on failure. ~ *Charles Kettering*

The greatest invention in the world is the mind of a child. ~ *Thomas Edison*

Discovery is seeing what everybody else has seen and thinking what nobody else has thought. ~ *Albert Szent-Gyorgi*

Never tell people how to do things. Tell them what to do and they will surprise you with their ingenuity. ~ *General George Patton*

Money never starts an idea; it is the idea that starts the money. ~ *William J. Cameron*

The way to succeed faster is to double your failure rate. ~ *Thomas Watson*

No idea is so outlandish that it should not be considered. ~ *Winston Churchill*

Conclusions arrived at through reasoning have very little or no influence in altering the course of our lives. ~ *Carlos Casteneda*

After years of telling corporate citizens to 'trust the system,' many companies must relearn instead to trust their people - and encourage their people to use neglected creative capacities in order to tap the most potent economic stimulus of all: idea power. ~ *Rosabeth Moss Kanter*

If you do not express your own original ideas, if you do not listen to your own being, you will have betrayed yourself. ~ *Rollo May*

Nothing is more dangerous than an idea when it is the only one you have. ~ *Emile Chartier*

There's always an element of chance and you must be willing to live with that element. If you insist on certainty, you will paralyze yourself. ~ *J.Paul Getty*

Almost all really new ideas have a certain aspect of foolishness when they are just produced. ~ *A.N. Whitehead*

The gift of fantasy has meant more to me than my talent for absorbing positive knowledge. ~ *Albert Einstein*

I've been doing a lot of abstract painting lately, extremely abstract. No brush, no paint, no canvas, I just think about it. ~ *Steven Wright*

Integrity

Integrity and commitment means if I say I will be at your house on Wednesday at three o'clock to paint your house for a dollar. I'm going to be there when I say I'll be there and I'm going to do what I say I will do ~ *Randy Risner, CEO of Silverado Painting Contractors.*

Nobody can acquire honor by doing what is wrong. ~ *Thomas Jefferson*

One has honor and integrity if he holds himself to an ideal of conduct though it is inconvenient, unprofitable, or dangerous to do so. ~ *Walter Lippmann*

Integrity without knowledge is weak and useless, and knowledge without integrity is dangerous and dreadful. ~ *Samuel Johnson*

The integrity of men is to be measured by their conduct, not by their professions. ~ *Junius*

A people that values its privileges above its principles soon loses both. ~ *Dwight David Eisenhower*

Lead your life so you wouldn't be ashamed to sell the family parrot to the town gossip. ~ *Will Rogers*

Character is doing the right thing when nobody's looking. There are too many people who think that the only thing that's right is to get by; and the only thing that's wrong is to get caught. ~ *J.C. Watts Jr.*

To give real service you must add something which cannot be bought or measured with money; and that is sincerity and integrity. ~ *Douglas Adams*

Have the courage to say no. Have the courage to face the truth. Do the right thing because it is right. These are the magic keys to living your life with integrity. ~ *W. Clement Stone*

J

Jealousy

In jealousy there is more self-love than love. ~ *François Rochefoucauld*

It is not love that is blind, but jealousy. ~ *Lawrence Durrell*

It is never wise to seek or wish for another's misfortune. If malice or envy were tangible and had a shape, it would be the shape of a boomerang. ~ *Charley Reese*

The jealous are troublesome to others, but a torment to themselves. ~ *William Penn*

Love looks through a telescope; envy, through a microscope. ~ *Josh Billings*

Envy is the art of counting the other fellow's blessings instead of your own. ~ *Harold Coffin*

Jealousy is simply and clearly the fear that you do not have value. Jealousy scans for evidence to prove the point that others will be preferred and rewarded more than you. There is only one alternative - self-value. If you cannot love yourself, you will not believe that you are loved. You will always think it's a mistake or luck. Take your eyes off others and turn the scanner within. Find the seeds of your jealousy, clear the old voices and experiences. Put all the energy into building your personal and emotional security. Then you will be the one others envy, and you can remember the pain and reach out to them. ~ *Jennifer James*

Jealousy in romance is like salt in food. A little can enhance the flavor, but too much can spoil the pleasure and, under certain circumstances, can be life-threatening. ~ *Maya Angelou*

Judging

Do not judge someone because they sin differently than you. ~ *Og Mandino*

People hasten to judge in order not to be judged themselves ~ *Albert Camus*

Never look down on anybody unless you're helping them up ~ *Jesse Jackson*

The highest form of human intelligence is to observe yourself without judgment ~ *Jiddu Krishnamurti*

When you're too religious, you tend to point your finger to judge instead of extending your hand to help ~ *Steve Maraboli*

Make no judgments where you have no compassion ~ *Anne Mcaffrey*

It strikes me there is something greater than judgment. I think it is called mercy ~ *Sebastian Berry*

Judge a man by his questions rather than his answers ~ *Voltaire*

If your busy judging people you have no time to love them ~*Mother Theresa*

Judgments prevent us from seeing the good that lies behind appearances ~ *Wayne Dyer*

Never judge a man's actions until you know his motives ~ *Paulo Coelho*

By judging others, you make yourself easy to judge ~ *Ashley Lorenzana*

K

Kindness

Kind words can be short and easy to speak, but their echoes are truly endless. ~ *Mother Teresa*

Give kindness to those you feel do not deserve it, they are most likely the ones who need it the most. ~ *Mary Angeline Gleed*

Today I bent the truth to be kind, and I have no regret, for I am far surer of what is kind than I am of what is true. ~ *Robert Brault*

If you haven't any charity in your heart, you have the worst kind of heart trouble. ~ *Bob Hope*

Today, give a stranger one of your smiles. It might be the only sunshine he sees all day. ~ *H. Jackson Brown Jr.*

Treat everyone with politeness, even those who are rude to you - not because they are nice, but because you are. ~ *Unknown*

Never miss an opportunity to make others happy, even if you have to leave them alone in order to do it. ~ *Unknown*

A fellow who does things that count, doesn't usually stop to count them. ~ *Albert Einstein*

Kindness is the language which the deaf can hear and the blind can see. ~ *Mark Twain*

Don't wait for people to be friendly, show them how. ~*Unknown*

Knowledge

Knowledge is like money, to be of value it must circulate, and in circulating it can increase in quantity and hopefully in value. ~ *Louis Lamour*

Knowledge has a beginning but no end. ~ *Geeta S. Iyengar*

The larger the island of knowledge, the longer the shoreline of wonder. ~ *Ralph W. Sockman*

Real knowledge is to know the extent of one's ignorance. ~ *Confucius*

In your thirst for knowledge, be sure not to drown in all the information. ~ *Anthony J. D'Angelo*

One part of knowledge consists in being ignorant of such things that are not worthy to be known. ~ *Crates*

The greatest obstacle to discovering the shape of the earth, the continents and the ocean was not ignorance but the illusion of knowledge. ~ *Daniel J. Boorstin*

Knowledge is the true organ of sight, not the eyes. ~ *Panchatantra*

We are here and now. Further than that, all knowledge is moonshine. ~ *H.L. Mencken*

If we would have new knowledge, we must get a whole world of new questions. ~ *Susanne K. Langer*

L

Law of Attraction

Everything that happens to you is a reflection of what you believe about yourself. We cannot outperform our level of self-esteem. We cannot draw to ourselves more than we think we are worth. ~ *Iyanla Vanzant*

Whatever it is you are feeling is a perfect reflection of what is in the process of becoming. ~ Rhonda Byrne

The person who sends positive thoughts activates the world around him positively and draws back to him positive results. ~ *Norman Vincent Peale*

The Law of Attraction states that all forms of matter and energy are attracted to that which is of a like vibration. The implications of this law are vast, and the law holds true for all known Universes. ~ *Abraham*

The universe works on many principles that are beyond our control. They work independent of our opinion about them and work even if we do not understand them. ~ *Wayne Dyer*

Your circumstances may be uncongenial, but they shall not remain so if you only perceive an ideal and strive to reach it. You cannot travel within and stand still without. ~ *James Allen*

Nurture your mind with great thoughts for you will never go higher than you think. ~ *Benjamin Disraeli*

Our job as humans is to hold on to the thoughts of what we want, make it absolutely clear in our minds what we want, and from that we start to invoke one of the greatest laws in the Universe, and that's the law of attraction. You become what you -

think about most, but you also attract what you think about most. ~ *John Assaraf*

What you think and what you feel and what manifest is always a match, every single time, no exceptions. ~ *Abraham Hicks*

The thoughts we hold attract similar thoughts and become large masses of thought called thought forms. The general vibration that a person holds is representative of the balance of their thoughts. ~ *Abraham*

It's really important that you feel good because feeling good is what goes out as a signal into the Universe and starts to attract more of itself to you, so the more you can feel good, the more you will attract the things that help you feel good and keep bringing you higher and higher. ~ *Joe Vitale*

I am not talking to you from the point of view of just wishful thinking, or imaginary craziness. I'm talking to you from a deeper basic understanding - quantum physics really begins to point to this discovery, it says that you can't have a universe without mind entering into it, the mind is actually shaping the very thing that is being perceived. ~ Fred Alan Wolf

As we become aware or conscious of our thoughts, we can raise our vibration by setting forth thoughts that are more in harmony with our desires. When our thoughts are in harmony with our highest desires, we are filled with joy and ecstasy. When we learn to set forth our thoughts consciously, we are no longer victims of our own outdated programming. We increasingly attract thought of a higher vibration and raise the level of thought at which we habitually vibrate. ~ *Abraham*

All of the great achievers of the past have been visionary figures; they were men and women who projected into the future. They thought of what could be, rather than what already was, and then they moved themselves into action, to bring these things into fruition. ~ Bob Proctor

The soul attracts that which it secretly harbors; that which it loves, and also that which it fears. ~ *James Allen*

You are never given a wish without also being given the power to make it true. You may have to work at it, however. ~ *Richard Bach*

In moments of powerful beauty, emotions move that can melt even the thickest and most cynical of skins. Endorphins flow. There is a release of tension. Energies, internal and external, flow and connect. The experience is not only soft and calm, but it also contains the power and creativity of nature and the universe. To create and to work consciously with these moments of connection is to exercise what we might call our spiritual muscles and our spiritual intelligence. What do I mean by spiritual? I simply mean that whole reality and dimension which is bigger, more creative, more loving, more powerful, more visionary, wiser, and more mysterious than materialistic daily known existence. ~ *William Bloom*

You might be thinking about past, or the present or the future, but whether you are remembering or observing or imagining, still in that process you are activating thought and law of attraction, which is the most powerful law in the universe, is responding to your thought. ~ *Abraham Hicks*

It has been proven now scientifically... an affirmative thought is a hundred times more powerful than a negative thought. ~ *Michael Beckwith*

Our subconscious minds have no sense of humor, play no jokes and cannot tell the difference between reality and an imagined thought or image. What we continually think about eventually will manifest in our lives. ~ *Robert Collier*

Whatever you create in your life you must first create in your imagination. ~ *Tycho Photiou*

As we increasingly master our perceptions, beliefs, thought and feeling patterns, we magnetically attract that which we most desire. ~ *Luanne Oakes*

I am no longer cursed by poverty because I took possession of my own mind, and that mind has yielded me every material thing I want, and much more than I need. But this power of mind is a universal one, available to the humblest person as it is to the greatest. ~ *Andrew Carnegie*

In your joy, you create something, and then you maintain your vibrational harmony with it, and the Universe must find a way to bring it about. That's the promise of Law of Attraction. ~ *Abraham Hicks*

Destiny is not a matter of chance; it is a matter of choice. ~ *William Jennings Bryan*

What lies behind us and what lies before us are tiny matters compared to what lies within us. ~ *Ralph Waldo Emerson*

By choosing your thoughts, and by selecting which emotional currents you will release and which you will reinforce, you determine the quality of your Light. You determine the effects that you will have upon others, and the nature of the experiences of your life. ~ *Gary Zukav*

You end up attracting to you the pre-dominant thoughts that you are holding in your awareness, whether those thoughts are conscious or whether they're unconscious. ~ *Michael Beckwith*

The law of attraction doesn't care whether you perceive something to be good or bad or whether you don't want it or you do want it, it's responding to your thoughts. ~ *Bob Doyle*

The greatest discovery of my generation is that human beings can alter their lives by altering their attitudes of mind. ~ *William James*

Go confidently in the direction of your dreams. Live the life you have imagined. ~ *Henry David Thoreau*

Every intention sets energy into motion, whether you are conscious of it or not. ~ *Gary Zukav*

Remember that your thoughts are the primary cause of everything. So, when you think a sustained thought it is immediately sent out into the Universe. That thought magnetically attaches itself to the like frequency, and then within seconds sends the reading of that frequency back to you through your feelings. Put another way, your feelings are communication back to you from the Universe, telling you what frequency you are currently on. Your feelings are your frequency feedback mechanism! ~ *Jack Canfield*

Live out of your imagination, not your history. ~ *Stephen Covey*

Your mind is a powerful magnet that will attract to you the things you identify yourself with. If you have sad thoughts, you will attract tragedies. If you are a good man, you will attract the company of good people. ~ *Alfredo Karras*

Laughter

Laughter is a tranquilizer with no side effects, take it regularly. ~ *Unknown*

At the height of laughter, the universe is flung into a kaleidoscope of new possibilities. ~ *Jean Houston*

Even if there is nothing to laugh about, laugh on credit. ~ *Unknown*

Sometimes I laugh so hard the tears run down my leg. ~ *Unknown*

Laughter is an instant vacation. ~ *Milton Berle*

Laughter is the shortest distance between two people. ~ *Victor Borge*

There is little success where there is little laughter. ~ *Andrew Carnegie*

What soap is to the body, laughter is to the soul. ~ *Yiddish Proverb*

A good, real, unrestrained, hearty laugh is a sort of glorified internal massage, performed rapidly and automatically. It manipulates and revitalizes corners and unexplored crannies of the system that are unresponsive to most other exercise methods. ~ *Maud van Buren*

A good laugh and a long sleep are the best cures in the doctor's book. ~ *Irish Proverb*

Laughter gives us distance. It allows us to step back from an event, deal with it and then move on. ~ *Bob Newhart*

I've always thought that a big laugh is a really loud noise from the soul saying. Isn't that the truth? ~ *Quincy Jones*

Remember, men need laughter sometimes more than food. ~ *Anna Fellows Johnston*

Leadership

Making a big life change is pretty scary, but you know what's even scarier? .... regret! ~ *Joshua Schneider*

Being a leader is like being a lady. If you have to remind people that you are, then you're not! ~ *Margaret Thatcher*

Your goal is to enable and empower people to make decisions independent of you. Each person on your team is an extension of your leadership. If they feel empowered by you, they will magnify your power to lead. ~ *Tom Ridge*

Deal with negative feelings head-on. Simmering resentment and anger are lethal to living your life on the highest plane. ~ *Graham Alexander*

Leadership is ultimately about creating a way for people to contribute to making something extraordinary happen. ~ *Alan Keith*

I have never in my life learned anything from any man who agreed with me. ~ *Dudley Field Malone*

The game plan tells you what you want to happen. But the scoreboard tells you what is happening. ~ *John Maxwell*

The ideas I stand for are not my own. I borrowed them from Socrates, I swiped them from Chesterfield, and I stole them from Jesus. And if you don't like their ideas, whose ideas would you rather use? ~ *Dale Carnegie*

The leader who wants to reach the top in business must appreciate the might of the force of habit, and he –

must understand that practices are what create habits. He must be quick to break those habits that can break him, and hasten to adopt those practices, that will become the habits that help him achieve the success he desires. ~ *J. Paul Getty*

The art of communication is the language of leadership. ~ *Ellen Hubbard*

If you realized how powerful our thoughts are, you would never think a negative thought. ~ *Peace Pilgrim*

The life which is unexamined is not worth living. ~ *Socrates*

Leaders should influence others in such a way that it builds people up, encourages and edifies them so they can duplicate this attitude in others. ~ *Bob Goshen*

Dump it, delegate, defer it, or do it! ~ *Jack Canfield*

Getting good players is easy, getting them to play together is the hard part. ~ *Casey Strengel*

Individual development is vital but will only get you so far, organizational level transformation requires a resonant and sustainable leadership culture, aligned high-performance teams, strong engagement, a commitment to system-wide learning and improvement and the unlocking of the collective intelligence. ~ *Peter Bluckert*

If your actions inspire others to dream more, learn more, do more and become more, you are leader. ~ *John Quincy Adams*

No one can be a great leader if he/she wants to do it all themselves or get all the credit for doing it. ~ *Andrew Carnegie*

Do not go where the path may lead, go instead where there is no path and leave a trail. ~ *Ralph Waldo Emmerson*

The biggest waste in any organization is the untapped potential of its people, and it's the job of leadership not HR to unleash it. ~ *Alame*

Wars may be fought with weapons, but they are won by men. It is the spirit of the men who follow and of the men who lead that gain the victory. ~ *George S. Patton*

Outstanding leaders go out of their way to boost the self-esteem of their personnel. If people believe in themselves, it's amazing what they can accomplish. ~ *Sam Walton*

Leadership is the capacity to translate vision into reality. ~ *Warren Bennis*

Good leaders create a vision, articulate the vision, passionately own the vision and relentlessly drive it to completion. ~ *Jack Welch*

Leadership is a serving relationship that has effect of facilitating human development. ~ *Ted Ward*

We have to ask ourselves, how do I go to work today and do something that will move the enterprise and myself another step in the right direction? ~ *Elaine Fortier*

Strange as it sounds, great leaders gain authority by giving it away. ~ *James Stockdale*

The more centers of leadership you find in a company, the stronger it will become. ~ *David Oglivey*

Leadership is learning by doing, adapting to actual situations. Leaders are constantly learning from their errors and failures. ~ *Claude Meyer*

We build strength and courage, and confidence by each experience in which we really stop to look fear in the –

face. We must do that which we think we cannot. ~ *Eleanor Roosevelt*

Press on ...... your defining moment may arrive just when you feel surrounded by adversity. ~ *David Cottrell*

If we are to truly invest in this generation of workers, we must offer a brain to pick, an ear to listen, a model to follow, and sometimes, a push in the right direction. ~ *Anonymous*

Being a good leader is not something that casually occurs, it takes great thought, care, insight, commitment, and energy. When it all comes together, it brings out the best of who you are. ~ *Mary Godwin*

Too often, we underestimate the power of a touch, a smile, a kind word, a listening ear, an honest compliment, or the smallest act of caring, all of which have the potential to turn a life around. ~ *Leo Buscaglia*

All things being equal, people will work with people they like, all things not being equal, they still will. ~ *John Maxwell*

Sustainable accountability is not inflicted, it's voluntary. ~ *Peter Chee*

A leader must create breathing room on a daily basis. ~ *Graham Alexander*

Be enthusiastic as a leader. You can't light a fire with a wet match. ~ *Oxford Leadership Academy*

Leaders become great, not because of their power, but for their ability to empower others. ~ *John Maxwell*

Everything you do, or leave undone, takes on greater meaning because of your position as a leader. ~ *Graham Alexander*

Innovation distinguishes between a leader and a follower. ~ *Steve Jobs*

Being the richest man in the cemetery doesn't matter to me, going to bed at night saying we've done something wonderful, that's what matters to me. ~ *Steve Jobs*

Any apology that doesn't accompany change is insult. ~ *Tessie Rose*

I'd rather change my mind and succeed then have my own way and fail. ~ *Emerson.*

Adversity unlocks virtue, defeat is the threshold of victory. ~ *Orison Sweet Marden*

Help those around you all you can. Every bit of help you give others will come back to you tenfold. ~ *E.B. Gallaher*

The secret of success is constancy of purpose. ~ *Desraeli*

There is no pillow as soft as a clear conscience. ~ *French Proverb*

God brings men into deep waters, not to drown them but to cleanse them. ~ *Aughery*

American organizations have been over managed and under led. ~ *Warren Bennis*

We ought to be able to learn some things second hand. There is not enough time to make all the mistakes ourselves. ~ *Harriet Hall*

Everyone has peak performance potential, you just need to know where they are coming from and meet them there. ~ *Ken Blanchard*

There is nothing so unequal as the equal treatment of unequal s. ~ *Ken Blanchard*

Learning

If you think education is expensive-try the cost of ignorance! ~ *Derek Bok*

A man's mind, once stretched by a new idea, never regains its original dimensions. ~ *Oliver Wendall Holmes*

You can teach a student a lesson for a day; but if you can teach him to learn by creating curiosity, he will continue the learning process as long as he lives. ~ *Clay P. Bedford*

I am learning all the time. The tombstone will be my diploma. ~ *Eartha Kitt*

The desire and hunger for education is the key to real learning. ~ *Jim Stovall*

It's what you learn after you know it all that counts. ~ *Attributed to Harry S Truman*

When the student is ready, the master appears. ~ *Buddhist Proverb*

Education consists mainly of what we have unlearned. ~ *Mark Twain*

The most useful piece of learning for the uses of life is to unlearn what is untrue. ~ *Antisthenes*

I find four great classes of students: The dumb who stay dumb. The dumb who become wise. The wise who go dumb. The wise who remain wise. ~ *Martin H. Fischer*

Anyone who stops learning is old, whether at twenty or eighty. ~ *Henry Ford*

Each day learn something new, and just as important, relearn something old. ~ *Robert Brault*

Linguistics

Words are the physicians of the mind. ~ *Aeschylus*

The words you choose to say something are just as important as the decision to speak. ~ *Anonymous*

The only weapon that becomes sharper with constant use is the tongue. ~ *Anonymous*

For me, words are a form of action, capable of influencing change. ~ *Ingrid Bengis*

Self-expression must pass into communication for its fulfillment. ~ *Pearl S. Buck*

Among my most prized possessions are words that I have never spoken. ~ *Orson Rega Card*

There are four ways, and only four ways, in which we have contact with the world. We are evaluated and classified by these four contacts: what we do, how we look, what we say, and how we say it. ~ *Dale Carnegie*

One of the basic causes for all the trouble in the world today is that people talk too much and think too little. They act impulsively without thinking. I always try to think before I talk. ~ *Margaret Chase Smith*

Language is a process of free creation; its laws and principles are fixed, but the manner in which the principles of generation are used is free and infinitely varied. Even the interpretation and use of words involves a process of free creation. ~ *Noam Chomsky*

Language is the armory of the human mind, and at once contains the trophies of its past and the weapons of its future conquests. ~ *Samuel Taylor Coleridge*

The individual's whole experience is built upon the plan of his language. ~ *Henri Delacroix*

Language is the blood of the soul into which thoughts run and out of which they grow. ~ *Oliver Wendell Holmes*

Language shapes the way we think, and determines what we can think about. ~ Benjamin Lee Whorf

A linguistic system is a series of differences of sound combined with a series of differences of ideas. ~ *Ferdinand De Saussure*

Always and never are two words you should always remember never to use. ~ *Wendell Johnson*

Words are, of course, the most powerful drug used by mankind. ~ *Rudyard Kipling*

It is better to keep one's mouth shut and be thought a fool than to open it and resolve all doubt. ~ *Abraham Lincoln*

He can compress the most words into the smallest ideas of any man I ever met. ~ *Abraham Lincoln*

Language is the inventory of human experience. ~ *L. W. Lockhart*

Listening

Silent" and "listen" are spelled with the same letters. ~ *Unknown*

My wife says I never listen to her. At least I think that's what she said. ~ *Unknown*

The most precious gift we can offer anyone is our attention. ~ *Thich Nhat Hanh*

A good listener is not only popular everywhere, but after a while he gets to know something. ~ *Wilson Mizner*

Don't worry that children never listen to you; worry that they are always watching you. ~ *Robert Fulghum*

An essential part of true listening is the discipline of bracketing, the temporary giving up or setting aside of one's own prejudices, frames of reference and desires so as to experience as far as possible the speaker's world from the inside, to step inside his or her shoes. ~ *M. Scott Peck, MD*

You never get people's fuller attention than when you're listening to them. ~ Robert Brault

The easiest way to meet people is to just look like someone who is willing to listen. ~ Robert Brault

It is the province of knowledge to speak and it is the privilege of wisdom to listen. ~ *Oliver Wendell Holmes*

Wisdom is the reward you get for a lifetime of listening when you'd have preferred to talk. ~ *Doug Larson*

We have two ears and one mouth so that we can listen twice as much as we speak. ~ *Epictetus*

Courage is what it takes to stand up and speak; courage is also what it takes to sit down and listen. ~ *Winston Churchill*

Losing

Sometimes it is better to lose and do the right thing than to win and do the wrong thing. ~ *Tony Blair*

Losing doesn't eat at me the way it used to. I just get ready for the next play, the next game, and the next season. ~ *Troy Aikman*

The greatest test of courage on earth is to bear defeat without losing heart. ~ *Robert G. Ingersoll*

Losing is no disgrace if you've given your best. ~ *Jim Palmer*

I get it now; I didn't get it then. That life is about losing and about doing it as gracefully as possible...and enjoying everything in between ~ *Mia Farrow*

Love

There is more hunger for love and appreciation in this world than for bread. ~ *Mother Teresa*

Love is a sacred reserve of energy; it is like the blood of spiritual evolution. ~ *Pierre Teilhard de Chardin*

To love and be loved is to feel the sun from both sides. ~ *David Viscott*

Accustom yourself continually to make many acts of love, for they kindle and melt the soul. ~ *Saint Teresa of Avila*

Love is a mutual self-giving which ends in self-recovery. ~ *Fulton J. Sheen*

It's useless to hold a person to anything he says while he's in love, drunk, or running for office ~ *Shirley MacLaine*

To love another person is to see the face of God. ~ *Victor Hugo*

Love is an act of endless forgiveness, and a tender look which becomes a habit. ~ *Peter Ustinov*

Romance is like maintaining a car. If you do a good job of it, you will always have a dependable quiet ride. ~ *T.R. Wallace*

Your task is not to seek for Love, but merely to seek and find all the barriers within yourself that you have built against it. ~ *Rumi*

How can a person give you so much strength, yet still be your only weakness? ~ *Anonymous*

Loyalty

There's loyalty that protects secrets and loyalty that protects truth. You cannot serve them both. ~ *Anonymous*

Loyalty is not a word, it's a life. ~ *Jim Rohn*

There's something wrong with your character if opportunity controls your loyalty. ~ *John Maxwell*

Loyalty to the country always, loyalty to the Government when it deserves it. ~ Mark Twain

Confidentiality is a virtue of the loyal, as loyalty is the virtue of faithfulness. ~ *Edwin Louis Cole*

A woman's loyalty is tested when her man has nothing. A man's loyalty is tested when he has everything. ~ *Anonymous*

Stand with anybody that stands right, stand with him when he is right and part with him when he is wrong. ~ *Abraham Lincoln*

Staying with someone who does not appreciate you isn't loyalty, its stupidity. ~ *Unknown*

Never let your loyalty become slavery, if they don't appreciate what you bring to the table, let them eat alone. ~ Unknown

M

Management

The world will not belong to managers or those who can make the numbers dance. The world will belong to passionate driven leaders, people who not only have enormous amounts of energy but who can energize those whom they lead. ~ *Jack Welch*

Make your top managers rich and they will make you rich. ~ *Robert H. Johnson*

You're only as good as the tools you're provided with. ~ *Amy Showalter*

If you pick the right people and give them the opportunity to spread their wings—and put compensation as a carrier behind it—you almost don't have to manage them. ~ *Jack Welch*

Everybody is a genius, but if you Judge a fish by its ability to climb a tree, it will live its whole life believing that it is stupid. ~ *Albert Einstein*

Time is the scarcest resource of a manager, if it is not managed, nothing else can be managed. ~ *Peter Drucker*

Roll your sleeves up and lead by example. If you're not willing to do the work neither will the people you manage. ~ *Amy Showalter*

Most of what we call management consists of making it difficult for people to get their work done. ~ *Peter Drucker*

Don't equate activity with efficiency. You are paying your key people to see the big picture. Don't let them get bogged down in a lot of meaningless meetings and paper shuffling. Announce a Friday afternoon off once in a while. Cancel a Monday morning meeting or two. Tell the cast of characters you'd like them to spend the amount of time normally spent preparing for attending the meeting at their desks, simply thinking about an original idea. ~ *Harvey Mackay*

Because a thing seems difficult for you, do not think it impossible for anyone else to accomplish. ~ *Marcus Aurelius*

We cling to hierarchies because our place in a hierarchy is rightly or wrongly, a major indicator of our social worth. ~ *Harold J. Leavitt*

Hire people who are better than you are, then leave them to get on with it. Look for people who will aim for the remarkable, who will not settle for the routine. ~ *David Ogilvy*

The secret of managing is to keep the guys who hate you away from the guys who are undecided. ~ *Casey Stengel*

A desk is a dangerous place from which to view the world. ~ *John Le Care*

Good management is the art of making problems so interesting and their solutions so constructive that everyone wants to get to work and deal with them. ~ *Paul Hawken*

I believe the real difference between success and failure in a corporation can be very often traced to the question of how well the organization brings out the great energies and talents of its people. ~ *Thomas J. Watson Jr.*

Focus on a few key objectives ... I only have three things to do. I have to choose the right people, allocate the right number of dollars, and transmit ideas from one division to another with the speed of light. So, I'm really in the business of being the gatekeeper and the transmitter of ideas. ~ *Jack Welch*

Management is, above all, a practice where art, science, and craft meet. ~ *Henry Mintzherg*

If you are the master, be sometimes blind, if you are the servant, be sometimes deaf. ~ *R. Buckminster Fuller*

The conventional definition of management is getting work done through people, but real management is developing people through work. ~ *Agha Hasan Abedi*

Manners

Etiquette means behaving yourself a little better than is absolutely essential. ~ *Will Cuppy*

Manners are a sensitive awareness of the feelings of others. If you have that awareness, you have good manners, no matter what fork you use. ~ *Emily Post*

Good manners will open doors that the best education cannot. ~ *Clarence Thomas*

Don't reserve your best behavior for special occasions. You can't have two sets of manners, two social codes - one for those you admire and want to impress, another for those whom you consider unimportant. You must be the same to all people. ~ *Lillian Eichler Watson*

The best index to a person's character is how a person treats people who can't do them any good or can't fight back. ~ *Abigail Van Buren*

Politeness and consideration for others is like investing pennies and getting dollars back. ~ *Thomas Sowell*

One of the greatest victories you can gain over someone is to beat him at politeness. ~ Josh Billings

Marketing

The aim of marketing is to know and understand the customer so well the product or service fits him and sells itself. ~ *Peter F. Drucker*

The sole purpose of marketing is to sell more to more people, more often and at higher prices. There is no other reason to do it. ~ *Sergio Zyman*

What really decides consumers to buy or not to buy is the content of your advertising, not its form. ~ *David Ogilvy*

Instead of one-way interruption, web marketing is about delivering useful content at precisely the right moment when a buyer needs it. ~ *David Meerman Scott*

The urgent can drown out the important. ~ *Marissa Mayer*

Because it is its purpose to create a customer, any business enterprise has two – and only these two ~ basic functions: marketing and innovation. - *Peter Drucker*

Don't find customers for your products, find products for your customers. ~ *Seth Godin*

Content is King! ~ *Bill Gates*

If you have more money than brains you should focus on *outbound* marketing. If you have more brains than money, you should focus on *inbound* marketing. ~ *Guy Kawasaki*

Markets are conversations. ~ *Levine, Locke, Searls and Weinberger*

What helps people, helps business. ~ *Leo Burnett*

Mastermind Principle

The mastermind principle consists of an alliance of two or more minds, working in perfect harmony for the attainment of a common definite objective. *~ Napoleon Hill*

No two minds ever come together without a third invisible force, which may be likened to a "third mind." When a group of individual minds are coordinated and function in harmony, the increased energy created through that alliance becomes available to every individual in the group. *- Napoleon Hill*

Mentoring

To accumulate wealth, you must study and emulate those who have acquired it before you. *~ Brian Tracy*

Apprentice for two years to a great, inspiring leader who'll mentor and teach you. Execute his or her requests with excellence and elegance. Meet and befriend all his or her friends, associates, bankers, clients, suppliers and actively keep them in your own Rolodex. *~ Mark Victor Hansen*

Example has more followers than reason. We unconsciously imitate what pleases us, and approximate to the characters we most admire. *~ Hristian Nevell Bovee*

No man is capable of self-improvement if he sees no other model but himself. *~ Conrado I. Generoso*

My mentor said, 'Let's go do it,' not 'you go do it.' How powerful when someone says, 'Let's! *~ Jim Rohn*

The mediocre teacher tells. The good teacher explains. The superior teacher demonstrates. The great teacher inspires. *~ William Arthur Ward*

Only mentor with successful people who care about you. *~ Rick Rea*

A mentor is someone who sees more talent and ability within you, than you see in yourself, and helps bring it out of you. ~ *Bob Proctor*

If you want to be successful, find someone who has achieved the results you want and copy what they do, and you'll achieve the same results. ~ *Anthony Robbins*

Delivering mentorship advice is like snow; the softer it falls, the longer it dwells upon, and the deeper it sinks into the mind. ~ *Samuel Taylor Coleridge*

The true secret of giving advice is, after you have honestly given it, to be perfectly indifferent whether it is taken or not and never persist in trying to set people right. ~ *Hannah Whitall Smith*

Tell me and I forget, teach me and I may remember, involve me and I learn. ~ *Benjamin Franklin*

Spoon feeding in the long run teaches us nothing but the shape of the spoon. ~ *E.M. Forster*

Metaphors

Metaphor provides a way to use representation and really piggyback our understanding of abstract concepts on the structure of concrete concepts. ~ *Sam Glucksberg*

A picture is worth a thousand words, but the right metaphor is worth a thousand pictures. ~ *Daniel Pink*

An individual's creation of metaphor is part of a fundamental human impulse to find meaning in life......through its capacity to clarify meaning in complex settings, metaphor is able to go beyond the limitations of scientific languages and descriptions. ~ *Eugene F. Provenzo Jr.*

Kant said that our metaphors comprise the conceptual spectacles through which we view the world. ... If we are to have meaningful, connected experiences; ones that we can comprehend and reason about; we must be able to discern patterns to our actions, perceptions, and conceptions. Underlying our vast network of interrelated literal meanings (all of those words about objects -

and actions) are those imaginative structures of understanding such as schema and metaphor, such as the mental imagery that allows us to extrapolate a path, or zoom in on one part of the whole, or zoom out until the trees merge into a forest. ~ *William H. Calvin*

The logic of the emotional mind is associative; it takes elements that symbolize a reality, or trigger a memory of it, to be the same as that reality. That is why similes, metaphors and images speak directly to the emotional mind. ... If the emotional mind follows this logic and its rules, with one element standing for another, things need not necessarily be defined by their objective identity: what matters is how they are perceived; things are as they seem. ... Indeed, in emotional life, identities can be like a hologram in the sense that a single part evokes a whole. ~ *Daniel Goleman*

Metaphor [is] a pervasive mode of understanding by which we project patterns from one domain of experience in order to structure another domain of a different kind. So conceived metaphor is not merely a linguistic mode of expression; rather, it is one of the chief cognitive structures by which we are able to have coherent, ordered experiences that we can reason about and make sense of. Through metaphor, we make use of patterns that we obtain in our physical experience to organize our more abstract understanding. ~ *Mark Johnson*

The power of metaphorical interventions may lie in the fact that metaphorical images are distributed throughout the brain in a holographic manner. If so, then exploring linguistic metaphors and early memory metaphors may activate this expansive network and transforming metaphors may reverberate throughout the entire range of distribution of the image and/or memory. ~ *Richard R Kopp*

We have discovered, over the past decade and a half, that a conceptual system contains an enormous subsystem of thousands of conceptual metaphors -- mappings that allow us to understand the abstract in terms of the concrete. Without this system, we could not engage in abstract thought at all -- in thought about causation, purpose, love, morality, or thought itself. Without the metaphor system, there could be no philosophizing, no theorizing, and little general understanding our everyday personal and social lives. But the operation of this vast system of conceptual metaphor is largely unconscious. We reason metaphorically throughout most of our waking, and even our dreaming lives, but for the most part are unaware of it. ~ *George Lakoff*

The challenge facing modern managers is to become accomplished in the art of using metaphor to find new ways of seeing, understanding, and shaping their actions. ~ *Gareth Morgan*

Miracles

If you don't believe in miracles, perhaps you've forgotten, "you are one." ~ *Og Mandino*

There are only two ways to live your life. One is as though nothing is a miracle. The other is as though everything is a miracle. ~ *Albert Einstein*

The miracles of nature do not seem to be miracles because they are so common. If no one had ever seen a flower, even a dandelion would be the most startling event in the world. ~ *Unknown*

Everything in your life is a miracle to be cherished. A grain of sand, a bee on a flower, a sailboat, a cup of coffee, a wet diaper, a caterpillar, are all miracles. When you learn to view life and everything in it as a miracle, you soon see that complaining is a waste of the miracle that you are. ~ *Wayne Dyer*

Miracles are not contrary to nature, but only contrary to what we know about nature. ~ *Saint Augustine*

103

Miracles happen every day, change your perception of what a miracle is, and you will see them all around you. ~ *Jon Bon Jovi*

Miracles are a retelling in small letters of the very same story which is written across the whole world in letters to large for some of us to see. ~ *C.S. Lewis*

Miracles occur naturally as an expression of love. The real miracle is the love that inspires them. In this sense everything that comes from love is a miracle. ~ Marianne Williamson

Positive thinking by itself does not work. Your embodied vision, partnered with vibrant thinking, harmonized with active listening, and supported with your conscious action - will clear the path for your Miracles. ~ *Summer Davenport*

The child must know that he is a miracle, that since the beginning of the world there hasn't been, and until the end of the world there will not be, another child like him. ~ *Pablo Casals*

Mistakes

To forget a mistake before seeking its lesson, condemns you to repeat it and thus relive its pain. ~ *Efram Ben-Jared*

I come from the school of thought that there is no such thing as a mistake - it is just a great learning experience. ~ *Unknown*

While one person hesitates because he feels inferior, the other is busy making mistakes and becoming superior. ~ *Henry C. Link*

Experience is that marvelous thing that enables you to recognize a mistake when you make it again. ~ *Franklin P. Jones*

To avoid situations in which you might make mistakes may be the biggest mistake of all. ~ Anonymous

A life spent making mistakes is not only more honorable, but more useful than a life spent doing nothing. ~ *George Bernard Shaw*

Mistakes, obviously, show us what needs improving. Without mistakes, how would we know what we had to work on? ~ *Peter McWilliams*

Success seems to be connected with action. Successful people keep moving. They make mistakes, but they don't quit. ~ *Conrad Hilton*

A well-adjusted person is one who makes the same mistake twice without getting nervous. ~ *Alexander Hamilton*

Modeling Behavior

Behavior is what a man does, not what he thinks, feels, or believes. ~ *Emily Dickinson*

In all things you yourself must be an example of good behavior. Be sincere and serious in your teaching. Use sound words that cannot be criticized, so that your enemies may be put to shame by not having anything bad to say about you. ~ *Titus 2:7-8*

Role modeling is the most basic responsibility of parents. Parents are handing life's scripts to their children, scripts that in all likelihood will be acted out for the rest of the children s lives. ~ *Stephen Covey*

You are in charge of your feelings, beliefs, and actions. And you teach others how to behave toward you. While you cannot change other people, you can influence them through your own behaviors and actions. By being a living role model of what you want to receive from others, you create more of what you want in your life. ~ *Eric Allenbaugh*

We simply assume that the way we see things is the way they really are or the way they should be. And our attitudes and behaviors grow out of these assumptions. ~ *Stephen Covey*

Money

If you want to feel rich just count the things you have that money can't buy. ~ *Unknown*

Money isn't everything, there is also hunger, misery and poverty. ~ Unknown

If you have a gun you can rob a bank, if you have a bank, you can rob everyone ~ *Bill Maher*

The real measure of your wealth is how much you would be worth if you lost all your money. ~ *Og Mandino*

Money is only used for two things. One, it's to make you comfortable, and the more comfortable you are the more creative you will become. And the other purpose is it enables you to extend the service you provide far beyond your own presence. ~ *Bob Proctor*

Money is only a tool. It will take you wherever you wish, but it will not replace you as the driver. ~ *Ayn Rand.*

Money won't create success, the freedom to make it will. ~ *Jim Rohn*

Successful people make money, it's not that people who make money become successful, but that successful people attract money. They bring success to what they do. ~ *Wayne Dyer*

Life is a game, money is how you keep score. ~ *Jim Rohn*

They say money does not bring you happiness, I say neither does being broke. ~ *P.T. Barnum*

Money and success don't' change people, they merely amplify what is already there. ~ *Will Smith*

The rate of interest acts as a link between income-value and cap-ital-value. ~ *Irving Fisher*

Your net worth to the world is usually determined by what remains after your bad habits are subtracted from your good ones. ~ *Benjamin Franklin*

Beware of little expenses, a small leak will sink a ship. ~ *Benjamin Franklin*

It is well enough that people of the nation do not understand our banking and monetary system, for if they did, I believe there would be a revolution before tomorrow morning. ~ *Henry Ford*

Financial literacy is an issue that should command our attention because many Americans are not adequately organizing finances for their education, healthcare and retirement. ~ *Ron Lewis*

The only way to permanently change the temperature in the room is to reset the thermostat. In the same way, the only way to change your level of financial success 'permanently' is to reset your financial thermostat. But it is your choice whether you choose to change. ~ *T. Harv Eker*

When your self-worth goes up, your net worth goes up with it. ~ *Mark Victor Hansen*

You must gain control over your money or the lack of it will forever control you. ~ *Dave Ramsey*

A big part of financial freedom is having your heart and mind free from worry about the what-ifs of life. ~ *Suze Orman*

It is a kind of spiritual snobbery that makes people think they can be happy without money. ~ *Albert Camus*

Being rich is a good thing. Not just in the obvious sense of benefitting you and your family, but in the broader sense. Profits are not a zero-sum game. The more you make, the more of a financial impact you can have. ~ *Mark Cuban*

art of your heritage in this society is the opportunity to become financially independent. ~ *Jim Rohn*

Managed money works harder and gives you a sense of destiny and purpose. ~ *Dave Ramsey*

The thing I have discovered about working with personal finance is that the good news is that it is not rocket science. Personal finance is about 80 percent behavior. It is only about 20 percent head knowledge. ~ *Dave Ramsey*

The size of your financial success is measured by the strength of your desire, the size of your dream and how you handle disappointment along the way. ~ *Robert Kyosaki*

In all realms of life, it takes courage to stretch your limits, express your power, and fulfill your potential. It's no different in the financial realm. ~ Suze Orman

Money is a mirror that reflects our personal strengths and weaknesses with great clarity. ~ *Unknown*

Money is like manure. You have to spread it around or it smells. ~ *J. Pal Getty*

Before you can transform your wallet from poor to rich, you've got to transform your spirit from poor to rich. ~ *Robert Kyosaki*

Those carrying a credit card balance should scale back to making the minimum payment each month, so they have more money to put into savings. ~ *Suze Orman*

Automating some of your finances can be incredibly convenient and is a great way to save time but automating everything makes it too easy to go on autopilot and forget to pay attention to your personal finances. ~ *Alexa Von Tobel*

N

Negativity

Many people who struggle with discontent are hell bent on keeping others down as well. It's a natural response but that doesn't mean you have to bend to it. ~ *Joshua Schneider*

Great people talk about ideas, average people talk about things, small people talk about other people. And even smaller people talk about themselves ~ *Eleanor Roosevelt*

One always looking for flaws leaves too little time for construction. ~ *Lewis F. Korns*

The best way of removing negativity is to laugh and be joyous. ~ *David Icke*

It is easier to avoid the effects of others' negativity when we question if an action or attitude is appropriately directed at us. If it isn't, we can choose to sidestep it and let it pass. ~ *Sue Patton Theole*

It's the simplest properties that will help you clear yourself of negativity ... The profound power of a simple prayer. The strength of a deep breath. The gentle guidance of good music. ~ *Jeffrey Wands*

Negativity is an addiction to the bleak shadow that lingers around every human form ... you can transfigure negativity by turning it toward the light of your soul. ~ *John O'Donohue*

Negativity can only feed on negativity. ~ *Elisabeth Kubler-Ross*

Dwelling on the negative simply contributes to its power. ~ *Shirley MacLaine*

Adopting the right attitude can convert a negative into a positive. ~ *Dr. Hans Selye*

Negotiating

The most difficult thing in any negotiation, almost, is making sure that you strip it of the emotion and deal with the facts. ~ *Howard Baker*

The fellow who says he'll meet you halfway usually thinks he's standing on the dividing line. ~ *Orlando A. Battista*

When a man says that he approves something in principal, it means he hasn't the slightest intention of putting it in practice. ~ *Otto Von Bismarck*

He who has learned to disagree without being disagreeable has discovered the most valuable secret of a diplomat. ~ *Robert Estabrook*

My father said: "You must never try to make all the money that's in a deal. Let the other fellow make some money too, because if you have a reputation for always making all the money, you won't have many deals. ~ *J. Paul Getty*

It is a trick among the dishonest to offer sacrifices that are not needed, or not possible, to avoid making those that are required. ~ *Ivan Goncharov*

In business, you don't get what you deserve, you get what you negotiate. ~ *Chester L. Karrass*

Prepare by knowing your walk away [conditions] and by building the number of variables you can work with during the negotiation... you need to have a walk away... a combination of price, terms, and deliverables that represents the least you will accept. Without one, you have no negotiating road map. ~ *Keiser*

During a negotiation, it would be wise not to take anything personally. If you leave personalities out of it, you will be able to see opportunities more objectively. ~ *Brian Koslow*

Flattery is the infantry of negotiation. ~ *Lord Chandos*

Never forget the power of silence, that massively disconcerting pause which goes on and on and may at last induce an opponent to babble and backtrack nervously. ~ *Lance Morrow*

You're in a much better position to talk with people when they approach you than when you approach them. ~ *Pilgrim, Peace*

Imaginative, sanguine men will never recognize that in negotiations the most dangerous moment of all is when everything is moving according to their wishes. ~ *Honore de Balzac*

Networking

The richest people in the world look for and build networks, everyone else looks for work. ~ *Robert T. Kiyosaki*

It's not what you know but who you know that makes the difference. ~ *Anonymous*

Networking is simply the cultivating of mutually beneficial, give and take, win-win relationships. It works best, however, when emphasizing the 'give' part. ~ *Bob Burg*

More business decisions occur over lunch and dinner than at any other time, yet no MBA courses are given on the subject. ~ *Peter Drucker*

The successful net-workers I know, the ones receiving tons of referrals and feeling truly happy about themselves, continually put the other person's needs ahead of their own. ~ *Bob Burg*

The currency of real networking is not greed but generosity. ~ *Keith Ferrazzi*

Poverty, I realized, wasn't only a lack of financial resources; it was isolation from the kind of people that could help you make more of yourself. ~ *Keith Ferrazzi*

Networking is an essential part of building wealth. ~ *Armstrong Williams*

O

Opportunity

Opportunity If opportunity doesn't knock, build a door. ~ *Milton Berle*

Jumping at several small opportunities may get us there more quickly than waiting for one big one to come along. ~ *Hugh Allen*

Opportunity is often difficult to recognize; we usually expect it to beckon us with beepers and billboards. ~ *William Arthur Ward*

Opportunities do not come with their values stamped upon them. ~ *Maltbie Babcock*

A wise man will make more opportunities than he finds. ~ *Francis Bacon*

Opportunities are never lost; someone will take the one you miss. ~ *Unknown*

Opportunity is a parade. Even as one chance passes, the next is a fife and drum echoing in the distance. ~ *Robert Brault*

A pessimist is one who makes difficulties of his opportunities and an optimist is one who makes opportunities of his difficulties. ~ *Harry Truman*

Optimism

Life is too short to spend your precious time trying to convince a person who wants to live in gloom and doom otherwise. Give lifting that person your best shot, but don't hang around long enough for his or her bad attitude to pull you down. Instead, surround yourself with optimistic people. ~ *Zig Ziglar*

Positive things happen to positive people. ~ *Sarah Beeny*

People who have drawn wealth into their lives used The Secret, whether consciously or unconsciously. They think thoughts of abundance and wealth, and they do not allow any contradictory thoughts to take root in their minds. ~ *Rhonda Byrne*

When you are asked if you can do a job, tell 'em, 'Certainly I can!' Then get busy and find out how to do it. ~ *Theodore Roosevelt*

A healthy attitude is contagious but don't wait to catch it from others. Be a carrier. ~ *Unknown*

When you live your life with an appreciation of coincidences and their meanings, you connect with the underlying field of infinite possibilities. ~ *Deepak Chopra*

You must not under any pretense allow your mind to dwell on any thought that is not positive, constructive, optimistic, kind. ~ *Emmet Fox*

Reflect upon your present blessings, of which every man has many, not on your past misfortunes, of which all men have some. ~ *Charles Dickens*

You can complain because roses have thorns, or you can rejoice because thorns have roses. ~ *Ziggy*

Whatever qualities the rich may have, they can be acquired by anyone with the tenacity to become rich. The key, I think, is confidence. Confidence and an unshakable belief it can be done and that you are the one to do it. ~ *Felix Dennis*

Organized

Don't agonize. Organize. ~ *Florence Kennedy*

Early in my career I felt that organization would destroy my creativity. Whereas now, I feel the opposite. Discipline is the concrete that allows you to be creative. - *Verna Gibson*

Good order is the foundation of all things. ~ *Edmund Burke*

Have a time and place for everything, and do everything in its time and place, and you will not only accomplish more, but have far more leisure than those who are always hurrying. ~ *Tryon Edwards*

However well organized the foundations of life may be, life must always be full of risks. ~ *Havelock Ellis*

I see something that has to be done and I organize it. ~ *Elinor Guggenheimer*

One person's mess is merely another person's filing system. ~ Margo *Kaufman*

Order is never observed; it is disorder that attracts attention because it is awkward and intrusive. ~ *Eliphas Levi*

Organize your life around your dreams - and watch them come true. ~ *Unknown*

Organizing is what you do before you do something, so that when you do it, it's not all mixed up. ~ *A.A. Milne*

P

Passion

The heart of human excellence often begins to beat when you discover a pursuit that absorbs you, frees you, challenges you, and gives you a sense of meaning, joy and passion. ~ *Unknown*

I have found that one thing that helps me to live peacefully and mindfully on this glorious planet is successful engagement in meaningful work that I am passionate about. ~ *Unknown*

It's not how much money you make that ultimately makes you happy. It's whether or not your work fulfills you. ~ *Unknown*

Neglecting passion blocks creative flow. When you're passionate, you're energized. Likewise, when you lack passion, your energy is low and unproductive. Energy is everything when it comes to being successful. ~ *Unknown*

When passion and skill work together, the end result is often a masterpiece. ~ *Unknown*

When we focus on leading a passionate, meaningful life, we are also inadvertently creating a spectacular ripple effect of inspiration in the lives around us. When one person follows a dream, tries something new, or takes a daring leap, everyone nearby feels their passionate energy; and before too long, they are making their own daring leaps while simultaneously inspiring others. ~ *Unknown*

As individuals we also have a sweet spot, where the response to our personal effort is maximized – the intersection of our gifts and passion with the proper opportunities. It is the zone that embodies the best or most effective use of our unique skills and abilities. ~ *Talayah G. Stovall*

Purpose is the reason you journey. Passion is the fire that lights your way. ~ *Unknown*

Only passions, great passions, can elevate the soul to great things. ~ *Unknown*

If you cannot put your heart in it, take yourself out of it. ~ Unknown

There are many things in life that will catch your eye, but only a few will catch your heart. ~ *Unknown*

Patience

A handful of patience is worth more than a bushel of brains. ~ *Dutch Proverb*

How can a society that exists on instant mashed potatoes, packaged cake mixes, frozen dinners, and instant cameras teach patience to its young? ~ *Paul Sweeney*

Patience is something you admire in the driver behind you and scorn in the one ahead. ~ *Mac McCleary*

Patience is the ability to count down before you blast off. ~ *Author Unknown*

Genius is nothing but a great aptitude for patience. ~ *George-Louis de Buffon*

Patience and perseverance have a magical effect before which difficulties disappear and obstacles vanish. ~ *John Quincy Adams*

Patience is the companion of wisdom. ~ *St. Augustine*

Patience is also a form of action. ~ *Auguste Rodin*

One moment of patience may ward off great disaster. One moment of impatience may ruin a whole life. ~ *Chinese Proverb*

Peace

The best way to pay for a lovely moment is to enjoy it. ~ *Richard Bach*

Spiritual energy brings peace and compassion into the world. ~ *Christina Baldwin*

Inner peace is beyond victory or defeat. ~ *Bhagavad Gita*

No man is free and at peace who is not master of himself. ~ *Epictetus*

When we have inner peace, we can be at peace with those around us. When our community is in a state of peace, it can share that peace with neighboring communities. ~ *Dalai Lama*

Acquire inner peace and a multitude will find their salvation near you. ~ *Catherine de Hueck Doherty*

Your thoughts are the architects of your destiny. ~ *David O. McKay*

The cyclone derives its powers from a calm center. So does a person. ~ *Norman Vincent Peale*

The true, or higher part of the self is always seeking the state that mystics talk about, the state in which we are filled with a universal love and a peaceful euphoria. ~ *James Redfield*

The most important of life's battles is the one we fight daily in the silent chambers of the soul. ~ *David O. McKay*

Performance

The fight is won or lost far away from the witnesses, behind the lines, in the gym, and out there on the road; long before I dance under those lights. ~ *Muhammad Ali*

When a team outgrows individual performance and learns team confidence, excellence becomes reality. ~ *Uknown*

Never lower your expectations to meet your performance, always raise your level of performance to meet your expectations. Expect the best of yourself and then do what is necessary to make it reality. ~ Ralph Marsten

Most of the important things in the world have been accomplished by people who have kept on trying when there seemed to be no hope at all. ~ *Dale Carnegie*

Great works are performed, not by strength, but by perseverance. ~ *Samuel Johnson*

The highest levels of performance come to people who are centered, intuitive, creative and reflective – people who know how to see a problem as an opportunity. ~ Deepak Chopra

The best way to inspire people to superior performance is to convince them by everything you do and by your everyday attitude that you are wholeheartedly supporting them. ~ Harold S. Geneen

Everything depends upon execution; having just a vision is no solution.
~ *Stephen Sondheim*

You can often outperform what other people think of you, but you will never outperform what you think of yourself. ~ *Jim Stovall (Author of "The Ultimate Gift)*

Great works are done when one is not calculating and thinking.
~ *Daisetz T. Suzuki*

A total commitment is paramount to reaching the ultimate in performance. ~ *Tim Flores*

It is not your aptitude, but your attitude, that determines your altitude. ~ *Zig Ziglar*

It is time for us to stand and cheer for the doer, the achiever, the one who recognizes the challenge and does something about it. ~ *Vince Lombardi*

To a brave man, good and bad luck are like his left and right hand. He uses both. ~ *St. Catherine of Siena*

Persistence

If you can't fly then run, if you can't run then walk, if you can't walk then crawl, but whatever you do you have to keep moving forward. ~ *Martin Luther King, Jr.*

A river cuts through rock, not because of its power, but because of its persistence. ~ *Jim Watkins*

There are two ways of attaining an important end, force and perseverance; the silent power of the latter grows irresistible with time. ~ *Sophie Swetchine*

Most people never run far enough on their first wind to find out they've got a second. ~ *William James*

Don't let the fear of the time it will take to accomplish something stand in the way of your doing it. The time will pass anyway; we might just as well put that passing time *to* the best possible use. ~ *Earl Nightingale*

What makes the difference between success and mediocrity? Sometimes it is just the willingness to hang in there. ~ *Talayah G. Stovall*

Success seems to be largely a matter of hanging on after others have let go. ~ *William Feather*

Be like a postage stamp. Stick to it until you get there. ~ *Bob Proctor*

Paralyze resistance with persistence. ~ *Woody Hayes*

All right Mister, let me tell you what winning means... you're willing to go longer, work harder, give more than anyone else. ~ *Vincent Lombardi*

Permanence, perseverance, and persistence in spite of all obstacles, discouragements and impossibilities; it is this that in all things distinguishes the strong soul from the weak. ~ *Thomas Carlyle*

Many of life's failures are people who did not realize how close they were to success when they gave up. ~ *Thomas Edison*

Personal Development

Someone has to have the awesome job, great car, huge smile on his face and interesting hobby, why not you? If it's not you it'll be your neighbor, co-worker or the guy who listened to himself when you didn't. ~ *Joshua Schneider*

Direct your thoughts, control your emotions and ordain your destiny. ~ W. *Clement Stone*

You have gifts and talents in a combination that no one else possesses. Don't deprive the world, and yourself by not utilizing your gift. ~ *Joshua Schneider*

A new philosophy, a new way of life, is not given for nothing. It has to be paid dearly for and only acquired with much patience and great effort. ~ *Fyodor Dostoivsky*

The state of your life is nothing more than the reflection of your state of mind. ~ *Wayne Dyer*

If you consistently invest in the neck up, you will never have to worry about the neck down. ~ *Zig Ziglar*

The first trait that is common among those who are assured a place in history is that of being predisposed to continual self-improvement. Those who have it are dynamically regenerative. ~ *James Stockdale*

It is one of the most beautiful compensations of life that no man can sincerely try to help another, without helping himself. ~ *Ralph Waldo Emerson*

One man cannot do right in one department of life while he is occupied in doing wrong in any other department. Life is one indivisible whole. ~ *Jim Rohn*

Change is inevitable but personal growth is a choice. ~ *Bob Proctor*

You decide your own fate, you steer your own ship. You can make the life you've always dreamed of happen, so get out of your own way and get dreaming. ~ *Joshua Schneider*

Those who bring sunshine into the lives of others cannot keep it from themselves. ~ *James Mathew Barrie*

Look what you can give back to the world, see where your voice can make the loudest noise, your hands a lasting impact, and truly change this world for your lifetime and beyond. ~ *Joshua Schneider*

Look up – See De-Light, look down- See De-Feet. ~ *Candace Cummings*

Keep away from people who belittle your ambition. Small people do that, but really great people make you feel like you too can become great. ~ *Mark Twain*

If God didn't want us to go forward, he would have put toes on our heels. ~ *Candace Cummings*

There are no such things as limits to growth, because there are no limits on the human capacity for intelligence, imagination and wonder. ~ *Ronald Reagan*

It's what you learn after you know it all that counts. ~ *John Wooden*

NEXTLEVEL is an intangible almost imperceptible growth – one that takes place inside of you. The result of personal growth is expanded intellect, and a shift in your mindset, belief system, and focus. ~ *Joshua Schneider* (Author of GENERATION NEXTLEVEL – The Twelve Laws)

If we don't change, we don't grow, if we don't grow, we aren't really living. ~ *Gail Sheehy*

You must take full responsibility, you cannot change the circumstances, the seasons, or the wind, but you can change yourself. ~ *Jim Rohn*

Intuition will tell the thinking mind where to look next. ~ *Dr. Jonas Salk*

Self-knowledge is learned not by contemplation, but by action. Strive to do your duty and you will soon discover of what stuff you are made of. ~ *Johann Goethe*

All that is necessary for the triumph of evil is that good men do nothing. ~ *Edmond Burke*

Taking baby steps may not feel like much now but spending 20 minutes thumbing through success magazine is going to get you a lot further than the same 20 minutes spent on facebook or sports highlights. ~ *Joshua Schneider*

There are some people who live in a dream world, and there are some who face reality; and then there are those who turn one into the other. ~ *Douglas H. Everett*

It is not the strongest of the species that survive, not the most intelligent, but the one most responsive to change. ~ *Charles Darwin*

Planning

Most people spend more time planning their summer vacation then planning their lives. ~ *Unknown*

The man who is prepared, has his battle half fought. ~ *Miguel de Cervantes*

A plan is a list of actions arranged in whatever sequence is thought likely to achieve an objective. ~ *John Argenti*

Plans are only good intentions unless they immediately degenerate into hard work. ~ *Peter Drucker*

It's not the plan that's important, it's the planning. ~ *Dr. Gramme Edwards*

By failing to prepare, you are preparing to fail. ~ *Benjamin Franklin*

A good plan is like a road map: it shows the final destination and usually the best way to get there. ~ *H. Stanely Judd*

Planning is bringing the future into the present so that you can do something about it now. ~ *Alan Lakein*

A good plan today is better than a perfect plan tomorrow. ~ *Geoge S. Patton*

Planning is a process of choosing among those many options. If we do not choose to plan, then we choose to have others plan for us. ~ *Richard I. Winwood*

Reduce your plan to writing. The moment you complete this, you will have definitely given concrete form to the intangible desire. ~ *Napoleon Hill*

Power

Power is the faculty or capacity to act, the strength and potency to accomplish something. It is the vital energy to make choices and decisions. It also includes the capacity to overcome deeply embedded habits and cultivate more effective ones. ~ *Stephen Covey*

Man was not made to bow in humiliation and shame, but to assert his divinity. He was made erect so that he could stand up and look anything and everything in the face. Even his maker, for he was made in his image. If man is a prince, if he has royal blood in his veins, if he has inherited the divine moral attributes, He should claim his birthright boldly and manfully, with dignity and assurance. ~ *James Allen*

The day the power of love overrules the love of power, the world will know peace. ~ *Mahatma Gandhi*

Nearly all men can stand adversity, but if you want to test a man's character, give him power. ~ *Abraham Lincoln*

Power does not corrupt. Fear corrupts. Perhaps the fear of a loss of power. ~ *John Steinbeck*

Washing one's hands of the conflict between the powerful and the powerless means to side with the powerful, not to be neutral. ~ *Paulo Freire*

Silence is the ultimate weapon of power. ~ *Charles de Gaulle*

It is said that power corrupts, but actually it's a truer statement would be that power attracts the corruptible. The sane are usually attracted by other things than power. ~ *David Brin*

Ultimately, the only power to which man should aspire is that which he exercises over himself. ~ *Elie Weisel*

For the powerful, crimes are those that others commit. ~ *Noam Chomsky*

We know that no one ever seizes power with the intention of relinquishing it. ~ *George Orwell*

Lust for power is a weed that grows only in the vacant lots of an abandoned mind. ~ *Ayn Rand*

The greater the power, the more dangerous the abuse. ~ *Edmund Burke*

With great power there must also come great responsibility! ~ *Stan Lee*

Absolute power was not meant for man. ~ *William E. Channing*

Mastering others is strength. Mastering yourself is true power. ~ *Tao Te Ching*

If you can abuse your power you have too much. ~ *Marty Rubin*

And power without compassion is the worst kind of evil there is. ~ *E.J. Patten*

The most common way people give up their power is by thinking they don't have any. ~ *Alice Walker*

Prayer

Do not pray for tasks equal to your powers, pray for powers equal to your tasks. ~ *Phillips Brooks*

The value of consistent prayer is not that He will hear us, but that we will hear Him. ~ *William McGill*

When we talk to God, we're praying. When God talks to us, we're schizophrenic. ~ *Jane Wagner*

We have to pray with our eyes on God, not on the difficulties. ~ *Oswald Chambers*

Prayer may not change things for you, but it for sure changes you for things. ~ *Samuel M. Shoemaker*

When a man is at his wits end it is not a cowardly thing to pray, it is the only way he can get in touch with Reality. ~ *Oswald Chambers*

Scientific prayer is the harmonious interaction of the conscious and subconscious levels of the mind, scientifically directed toward a specific purpose. ~ *Joseph Murphy*

Many people pray as if God were a big aspirin pill; they come only when they hurt. ~ *B. Graham Dienert*

Some have been to the mountain. I have been to my knees by the side of my bed. ~ *Robert Brault*

Prayer is when you talk to God; meditation is when you listen to God. ~ *Author Unknown*

Prayer is not merely an occasional impulse to which we respond when we are in trouble: prayer is a life attitude. ~ *Walter A. Mueller*

Prayer is to unite mentally and emotionally with the goodness you wish to embody. ~ *Joseph Murphy*

Prayer gives a man the opportunity of getting to know a gentleman he hardly ever meets. I do not mean his maker, but himself. ~ *William Inge*

Grow flowers of gratitude in the soil of prayer. ~ *Terri Guillemets*

Prayer requires more of the heart than of the tongue. ~ *Adam Clarke*

God speaks in the silence of the heart. Listening is the beginning of prayer. ~ *Mother Teresa*

When you bow deeply to the universe, it bows back; when you call out the name of God, it echoes inside you. ~ *Morihei Ueshiba*

Most people do not pray; they only beg. ~ *George Bernard Shaw*

Prayer draws us near to our own souls. ~ *Herman Melville*

Prayer is more than meditation. In meditation, the source of strength is one's self. When one prays, he goes to a source of strength greater than his own. ~ *Anne Louise Germaine de Staël-Holstein*

We must move from asking God to take care of the things that are breaking our hearts, to praying about the things that are breaking His heart. ~ *Margaret Gibb*

Some people think that prayer just means asking for things, and if they fail to receive exactly what they asked for, they think the whole thing is a fraud. ~ *Gerald Vann*

God has editing rights over our prayers. He will... edit them, correct them, bring them in line with His will and then hand them back to us to be resubmitted. ~ *Stephen Crotts*

Be thankful that God's answers are wiser than your answers. ~ *William Culbertson*

Prayer is exhaling the spirit of man and inhaling the spirit of God. ~ *Edwin Keith*

The Lord longs to hear all of our concerns - any concern too small to be turned into a prayer is too small to be made into a burden. ~ *Corrie Ten Boom*

Principles

Great ambition is the passion of a great character. Those endowed with it may perform very good or very bad acts. All depends on the principles which direct them. ~ *Napoleon Bonaparte*

Don't try to be different. Just be good. To be good is different enough. ~ *Arthur Freed*

There are three constants in life... change, choice and principles. ~ *Stephen Covey*

Do not repeat anything you will not sign your name to. ~ *Author Unknown*

I love those who can smile in trouble, who can gather strength from distress, and grow brave by reflection. Tis the business of little minds to shrink, but they whose heart is firm, and whose conscience approves their conduct, will pursue their principles unto death. ~ *Leonardo da Vinci*

Every job is a self-portrait of the person who does it. Autograph your work with excellence. ~ *Author Unknown*

Laws control the lesser man. Right conduct controls the greater one. ~ *Unknown*

Failure comes only when we forget our ideals and objectives and principles. ~ Jawaharlal Nehru

A man has to live with himself, and he should see to it that he always has good company. ~ *Charles Evans Hughes*

My guiding principles in life are to be honest, genuine, thoughtful and caring. ~ *Prince William*

You do not wake up one morning a bad person. It happens by a thousand tiny surrenders of self-respect to self-interest. ~ *Robert   Brault*

You can out-distance that which is running after you, but not what is running inside you. ~ *Rwandan Proverb*

Better keep yourself clean and bright; you are the window through which you must see the world. ~ *George Bernard Shaw*

To know what is right and not do it is the worst cowardice. ~ *Confucius*

Proper principle is doing the right thing even when it costs more than you want to pay. ~ *Michael Josephson*

The principles of living greatly include the capacity to face trouble with courage, disappointment with cheerfulness, and trial with humility. ~ *Thomas S. Monson*

Just do good, don't worry about the road ahead. ~ *Monk Wansong*

I am, indeed, a king, because I know how to rule myself. ~ *Pietro Aretino*

An army of principles can penetrate where an army of soldiers cannot. ~ *Thomas Paine*

People who fight fire with fire end up with only the ashes of their own integrity. ~ *Michael Josephson*

A people that values its privileges above its principles soon loses both. ~ *Dwight D. Eisenhower*

Conscience is that still, small voice that is sometimes too loud for comfort. ~ *Bert Murray*

Live in such a way that you would not be ashamed to sell your parrot to the town gossip. ~ *Will Rogers*

Problem Solving

The significant problems we face cannot be solved on the same level of thinking we were at when we created them. ~ *Albert Einstein.*

One might as well try to ride two horses moving in different directions, as to try to maintain, in equal force, two opposing or contradictory sets of desires. ~ *Robert Collier.*

The difference between a 30,000.00 a year earner and a million dollar a year earner is attitude and how you deal with problems. ~ *Unknown*

Problems are to the mind, what exercise is to the muscles, they toughen and make us strong. ~ *Norman Vincent Peale*

If I had 20 days to solve a problem, I would take 19 days to define it. ~ *Albert Einstein*

All the greatest and most important problems of life are fundamentally insolvable. They can never be solved, but only outgrown. ~ *Carl Jung*

Problems can only be avoided by exercising good judgment. Good judgment can only be gained by experiencing life's problems. ~ *Jim Stovall*

The biggest problem in the world could have been solved when it was small. ~ *Wittier Bynner*

A clever person solves a problem. A wise person avoids it. ~ *Albert Einstein*

Don't dwell on what went wrong. Instead, focus on what to do next. Spend your energies on moving forward toward finding the answer. ~ *Denis Waitley*

Don't hope for a life without problems. An easy life results in a judgmental and lazy mind. ~ *Kyong Ho*

Every problem contains within itself the seeds of its own solution. ~ *Stanley Arnold*

For every complex problem, there is a solution that is simple, neat, and wrong. ~ *H.L. Mencken*

I once asked God what I could give him. "Your problems," he said. "I've got everything else. ~ *Lionel Blue*

If you can't solve it, it's not a problem--its reality. ~ *Barbara Colorose*

If you can talk brilliantly about a problem, it can create the consoling illusion that it has been mastered. ~ *Stanley Kubrick*

It is well known that "problem avoidance" is an important part of problem solving. Instead of solving the problem you go upstream and alter the system so that the problem does not occur in the first place. ~ *Edward de Bono*

It is wise to direct your anger towards problems--not people; to focus your energies on answers--not excuses. ~ *William Arthur Ward*

The man who has no more problems to solve is out of the game. ~ *Elbert Hubbard*

The problem is not that there are problems. The problem is expecting otherwise and thinking that having problems is a problem. ~ *Theodore Ruskin*

Recognizing a problem is the first step to solving it... Some problems cannot be solved but you can make peace with them. ~ *Sanya Friedman*

Responsibility is the most powerful internal motivator for problem solving. When you remove it, all that remains is the lesser drive of self-preservation. If necessity is the mother of invention, then responsibility is its father. ~ *Mark A. Crouch*

Solving one problem always uncovers new problems that we could not have discovered before; answering one question inevitably leads us to new and better questions. ~ *LLN*

Sometimes the situation is only a problem because it is looked at in a certain way. Looked at in another way, the right course of action may be so obvious that the problem no longer exists. ~ *Edward de Bono*

Success is relevant to coping with obstacles... But no problem is ever solved by those, who, when they fail, look for someone to blame instead of something to do. ~ *Fred Waggoner*

There are two ways of meeting difficulties: You alter the difficulties, or you alter yourself to meet them. ~ *Phyllis Bottome*

To solve any problem, here are three questions to ask yourself: First, what could I do? Second, what could I read? And third, who could I ask? ~ *Jim Rohn*

Too often we give our children answers to remember rather than problems to solve. ~ *Roger Lewin*

When fog prevents a small-boat sailor from seeing the buoy marking the course he wants, he turns his boat rapidly in small circles, knowing that the waves he makes will rock the buoy in the vicinity. Then he stops, listens and repeats the procedure until he hears the buoy clang. By making waves, he finds where his course lies... Often the price of finding these guides is a willingness to take a few risks, to "make a few waves." A boat that stays in the harbor never encounters dangers--but it also never gets anywhere. ~ *Richard Armstrong*

131

Procrastination

You can transform something important into something urgent if you wait long enough. *~ Unknown*

Nothing is so fatiguing as the eternal hanging on of an uncompleted task. *~ William James*

Procrastination is the art of keeping up with yesterday. *~ Don Marquis*

Until you value yourself, you will not value your time. Until you value your time, you will not do anything with it. *~ Scott Peck*

If you want to make an easy job seem mighty hard, just keep putting off doing it. *~ Olin Miller*

There are a million ways to lose a work day, but not even a single way to get one back. *~ Tom DeMarco*

It is an undoubted truth, that the less one has to do, the less time one finds to do it in. *~ Earl of Chesterfield*

Work expands so as to fill the time available for its completion. *~ C. Northcote Parkinson*

Procrastination is opportunity's natural assassin. *~ Victor Kiam*

What may be done at any time will be done at no time. *~ Scottish Proverb*

Procrastination is something best put off until tomorrow. *~ Gerald Vaughan*

The best way to get something done is to begin. *~ Author Unknown*

Never put off until tomorrow what you can do the day after tomorrow. *~ Mark Twain*

Procrastination is the bad habit of putting off until the day after tomorrow what should have been done the day before yesterday. *~ Napoleon Hill*

Procrastination is, hands down, our favorite form of self-sabotage. ~ *Alyce P. Cornyn-Selby*

Procrastination is the grave in which opportunity is buried. ~ *Unknown*

Procrastination is suicide on the installment plan. ~ *Unknown*

Procrastination is one of the most common and deadliest of diseases and its toll on success and happiness is heavy. ~ *Wayne Dyer*

Profanity

The foolish and wicked practice of profane cursing and swearing is a vice so mean and low that every person of sense and character detests and despises it. ~ *George Washington*

I had three rules for my players: No profanity. Never criticize a team mate. Always be on time. ~ *John Wooden*

We don't do drugs, drink or use profanity. Instead we instill morals and values in my boys with a love of God and a love and respect for themselves and all people. ~ *Anita Baker*

Profanity is the effort of a feeble brain to express itself forcibly. ~ *Spencer Kimball*

Profanity is the lazy minds emotional expression of being inarticulate due to a small vocabulary ~ *Daniel Gleed*

Profaneness is a brutal vice. He who indulges in it is no gentleman. ~ *Edwin Hubble Chapin*

The higher a man stands, the more the word vulgar becomes unintelligible to him. ~ *John Ruskin*

Profanity, which is ever blasphemy against the divine beauty in life... is a monster for which the corruption of society forever brings forth new food, which it devours in secret. ~ *Albert Einstein*

The foolish and wicked practice of profane cursing and swearing is a vice so mean and low that every person of sense and character detests and despises it. ~ *George Washington*

Of all the dark catalogue of sins there is not one more vile and execrable than profaneness. ~ Samuel H. Cox

From a common custom of swearing, people easily slide into perjury; therefore, if thou wouldst not be perjured, do not lower thyself to swear. ~ *Hierocles*

Let thy speech be better than silence or else be silent. ~ *Dionysius of Halicarnassus*

Words are sacred. They deserve respect. If you get the right ones, in the right order, you can nudge the world a little. ~ *Tom Stoppard*

To swear is neither brave, polite, nor wise. ~ *Alexander Pope*

Prosperity

To dream anything that you want to dream. That's the beauty of the human mind. To do anything that you want to do. That is the strength of the human will. To trust yourself to test your limits. That is the courage to succeed. ~ *Bernard Edmonds*

Both adversity and prosperity can make fools out of people, prosperity makes more fools than adversity. ~ *Hubbard*

When it is obvious that the goals cannot be reached, don't adjust the goals; adjust the action steps. ~ *Confucius*

The more intensely we feel about an idea or a goal, the more assuredly the idea, buried deep in our subconscious, will direct us along the path to its fulfillment. ~ *Earl Nightingale*

You control your future, your destiny. What you think about comes about. By recording your dreams and goals on paper, you set in motion the process of becoming the person you most want to be. Put your future in good hands – your own. ~ *Mark Victor Hansen*

Success means having the courage, the determination, and the will to become the person you believe you were meant to be. ~ *George Sheehan*

Prosperity demands of us more prudence and moderation than adversity. ~ *Cicero*

Don't wait until everything is just right. It will never be perfect. There will always be challenges, obstacles and less than perfect conditions. So, what. Get started now. With each step you take, you will grow stronger and stronger, more and more skilled, more and more self-confident and more and more successful. ~ *Mark Victor Hansen*

Be at war with your vices, at peace with your neighbors, and let every New Year find you a better man. ~ *Benjamin Franklin*

Today's patience can transform yesterday's discouragements into tomorrow's discoveries. Today's purposes can turn yesterday's defeats into tomorrow's determination. ~ *William Arthur Ward*

Do not lose hold of your dreams or aspirations. For if you do, you may still exist, but you have ceased to live. - *Henry David Thoreau*

Life is a challenge, meet it! Life is a dream, realize it! Life is a game, play it! Life is love, enjoy it! ~ *Sri Sathya Sai Baba*

The increase of a great number of citizens in prosperity is a necessary element to the security, and even to the existence, of a civilized people. ~ *Buret*

Public Relations

It is always a risk to speak to the press: They are likely to report what you say. ~ *Hubert H. Humphrey*

If I was down to my last dollar, I would spend it on public relations. ~ *Bill Gates*

The public is the only critic whose opinion is worth anything at all. ~ *Mark Twain*

A lightweight, by definition, is a man who cannot assert his authority over the national press, cannot manipulate reporters, cannot finesse questions, prevent leaks or command a professional public relations operation. ~ *Unknown*

Everything you do or say is public relations. ~ *Anonymous*

Many have a misconception that public relations is all about spin. The truth of the matter is, effective public relations is all about balance. It's the fine art of delivering information, changing opinions, and shaping perceptions. Great PR is not about getting names into newspapers, it's about getting messages into minds. ~ Ogilvy PR

Public relations specialists make flower arrangements of the facts, placing them so that the wilted and less attractive petals are hidden by sturdy blooms. ~ *Alan Harrington*

Some are born great, some achieve greatness, and some hire public relations officers. ~ *Donald Trump*

In almost every act of our lives, whether in the sphere of politics or business, in our social conduct or our ethical thinking, we are dominated by the relatively small number of persons who understand the mental processes and social patterns of the masses. It is they who pull the wires that control the public mind. ~ *Edward Bernays*

Public relations is about reputation - the result of what you do, what you say and what others say about you... Public relations practice is the discipline which looks after reputation with the aim of earning understanding and support and influencing opinion and behavior. ~ *Institute of Public Relations*

Inasmuch as reputation affects marketing, public relations has a key part to play in the marketing mix. It also can have a crucial role in communicating an organization's corporate objectives to key audiences and may form an integral part of the management function, enhancing internal [employee] and external relationships. Good PR thus can have a significant contribution to a company's competitiveness and overall market position. ~ *Department for Trade and Industry*

Public relations is the planned and sustained effort to establish and maintain goodwill and mutual understanding between an organization and its public. ~ *Institute of Public Relations*

No word was ever as effective as a rightly timed pause. ~ *Mark Twain*

The questions don't do the damage. Only the answers do. ~ *Sam Donaldson*

Public Speaking

A mediocre speech supported by all the power of delivery will be more impressive than the best speech unaccompanied by such power. ~ *Quintilian*

Three things matter in a speech: who says it, how they say it, and what they say - and of the three, the last matters least. ~ *John Morley*

It usually takes more than three weeks to prepare a good impromptu speech. ~ *Mark Twain*

It is better to speak from a full heart and an empty head than from a full head and an empty heart. ~ *Dianna Daniels Booher*

The eloquent man is he who is no beautiful speaker, but who is inwardly and desperately drunk with a certain belief. ~ *Ralph Waldo Emerson*

Political speeches are like steer horns. A point here, a point there, and a lot of bull in between. ~ *Alfred E. Neuman*

Public speaking is the art of diluting a two-minute idea with a two-hour vocabulary. ~ *Evan Esar*

His speeches to an hour-glass, do some resemblance show, because the longer time they run the shallower they grow. ~ *Author Unknown*

The problem with speeches isn't so much not knowing when to stop, as knowing when not to begin. ~ *Frances Rodman*

A speech is like a woman's skirt: it needs to be long enough to cover the subject matter but short enough to hold the audience's attention. ~ *Author Unknown*

Commencement speeches were invented largely in the belief that outgoing college students should never be released into the world until they have been properly sedated. ~ *G.B. Trudeau*

Purpose

Power is released when the purpose is clear. ~ *Stevenson Willis*

A purpose has been granted unto all who walk the earth, but only those who seize the opportunities which conceal it will discover the road which leads to its fulfillment. ~ *Efram Ben-Jared*

Where your talent and the needs of the world cross, you're calling can be found. ~ *Aristotle*

Until thought is linked with purpose, there is no intelligent accomplishment. ~ *James Allen*

When we acknowledge that all life is sacred and that each act is an act of choice and, therefore, sacred, then life is a sacred dance lived consciously each moment. When we live at this level, we participate in the creation of a better world. ~ *Scout Cloud Lee*

There is a purpose to our lives that each day tugs at our sleeve as an annoying distraction. ~ *Robert Brault*

We all possess the thunder of pure fury and the calm breeze of tranquility. If it wasn't for tomorrow, how much would we get done today? Whatever your purpose... embrace it completely. Get lost in the clouds every now and then so you never lose sight of God's wonder. ~ *Paul Vitale*

Never ask, what reason do I have to be happy? Instead ask, to what purpose can I attach my happiness? ~ *Robert Brault*

This is the true joy in life, the being used for a purpose recognized by yourself as a mighty one; the being thoroughly worn out before you are thrown on the scrap heap; the being a force of nature instead of a feverish selfish little clod of ailments and grievances complaining that the world will not devote itself to making you happy. ~ *George Bernard Shaw*

Q

Quality

Almost all quality improvement comes via simplification of design, manufacturing, layout, processes, and procedures. ~ *Tom Peters.*

Be a yardstick of quality. Some people aren't used to an environment where excellence is expected. ~ *Steve Jobs*

Quality has to be caused, not controlled. ~ *Philip Crosby*

Quality in a product or service is not what the supplier puts in. It is what the customer gets out and is willing to pay for. ~ *Peter Drucker*

Quality is never an accident; it is always the result of high intention, sincere effort, intelligent direction and skillful execution; it represents the wise choice of many alternatives. ~ *William A. Foster*

Quality is not an act, it is a habit. ~ *Aristotle*

Quality is the result of a carefully constructed cultural environment. It has to be the fabric of the organization, not part of the fabric. ~ *Philip Crosby*

Quality means doing it right when no one is looking. ~ *Henry Ford*

Questions

There are no right answers to wrong questions. ~ *Ursula K. Le Guin*

What people think of as the moment of discovery is really the discovery of the question. ~ *Jonas Salk*

How do you know so much about everything? Was asked of a very wise and intelligent man; and the answer was, by never being afraid or ashamed to ask questions as to anything of which I was ignorant. ~ *John Abbott*

What we observe is not nature itself, but nature exposed to our method of questioning. ~ *Werner Heisenberg*

Ask the right questions if you're going to find the right answers. ~ *Vanessa Redgrave*

In all affairs, it's a healthy thing now and then to hang a question mark on the things you have long taken for granted. ~ *Bertrand Russell*

Judge a man by his questions rather than his answers. ~ *Voltaire*

We hear only those questions for which we are in a position to find answers. ~ *Friedrich Nietszche*

I don't pretend we have all the answers. But the questions are certainly worth thinking about. ~ *Arthur C. Clarke*

A wise man's question contains half the answer. ~ *Solomon Ibn Gabirol*

The power to question is the basis of all human progress. ~ *Indira Gandhi*

There is frequently more to be learned from the unexpected questions of a child than the discourses of men. ~ *John Locke*

How do you get the right answers? By asking the right questions, of course. The questions you ask define the areas in which you will look, so taking time and even asking questions about the questions you are asking can be a useful strategy for getting creatively great solutions. ~ *Jamie McKenzie*

Questioning is to thinking as yeast is to bread making. ~ *Napoleon Hill*

Questioning is what converts the stuff of thinking into something of value. ~ *Jamie McKenzie*

Everything we know has its origin in questions. Questions, we might say, are the principal intellectual instruments available to human beings. ~ *Alfred A. Knopf*

The test of a good teacher is not how many questions he can ask his pupils that they will answer readily, but how many questions he inspires them to ask him which he finds it hard to answer. ~ *Alice Wellington Rollins*

Asking the right questions takes as much skill as giving the right answers. ~ *Robert Half*

Quitting

Once you learn to quit, it becomes a habit. ~ *Vince Lombardi*

Doing nothing is the most tiresome job in the world because you cannot quit and rest. ~ *Unknown*

It's always too early to quit. ~ *Norman Vincent Peale*

Most people give up just when they're about to achieve success. They quit on the one-yard line. They give up at the last minute of the game, one foot from a winning touchdown. ~ *Ross Perot*

I've always made a total effort, even when the odds seemed entirely against me. I never quit trying; I never felt that I didn't have a chance to win. ~ *Arnold Palmer*

Success seems to be connected with action. Successful people keep moving. They make mistakes, but they don't quit. ~ *Conrad Hilton*

Effort only fully releases its reward after a person refuses to quit. ~ *Napoleon Hill*

Whenever you make a mistake or get knocked down by life, don't look back at it too long. Mistakes are life's way of teaching you. ~ *Og Mandino*

Winners are not those who never fail, but those who never quit. – Unknown

People of mediocre ability sometimes achieve outstanding success because they don't know when to quit. Most men succeed because they are determined to. ~ *George Allen*

R

Rapport

For most women, the language of conversation is primarily a language of rapport: a way of establishing connections and negotiating relationships. ~ *Deborah Tannen*

Here is one of the best bits of advice ever given about the fine art of human relationships. If there is any one secret of success, it lies in the ability to get the other person's point of view and see things from that person's angle as well as from your own. ~ *Henry Ford*

It's the individual who is not interested in his fellow man who has the greatest difficulties in life and provides the greatest injury to others. It is from among such individuals that all human failures spring. ~ *Lou Ferrigno*

When dealing with people, let us remember we are not dealing with creatures of logic. We are dealing with creatures of emotion, creatures bustling with prejudices and motivated by pride and vanity. ~ *Dale Carnegie*

You can make more friends in two months by becoming interested in other people than you can in two years by trying to get other people interested in you. ~ *Benjamin Franklin*

I am convinced now that nothing good is accomplished and a lot of damage can be done if you tell a person straight out that he or she is wrong. You only succeed in stripping that person of self-dignity and making yourself an unwelcome part of any discussion. ~ *Anonymous*

If you can inspire the people with whom you come in contact to a realization of the hidden treasures they possess, we can do far more than change people. You can literally transform them. ~ *Unknown*

Reading

A book is the only place in which you can examine a fragile thought without breaking it or explore an explosive idea without fear it will go off in your face. It is one of the few havens remaining where a man's mind can get both provocation and privacy. ~ *Edward P. Morgan*

I would be most content if my children grew up to be the kind of people who think decorating consists mostly of building enough bookshelves. ~ *Anna Quindlen*

Books are the quietest and most constant of friends; they are the most accessible and wisest of counselors, and the most patient of teachers. ~ *Charles W. Eliot*

Always read something that will make you look good if you die in the middle of it. ~ *P.J. O'Rourke*

I find television to be very educating. Every time somebody turns on the set, I go in the other room and read a book. ~ *Groucho Marx*

The man who does not read good books has no advantage over the man who can't read them. ~ *Mark Twain*

Let books be your dining table, and you shall be full of delights. Let them be your mattress and you shall sleep restful nights. ~ *Unknown*

I know every book of mine by its smell, and I have but to put my nose between the pages to be reminded of all sorts of things. ~ *George Robert Gissing*

Books let us into their souls and lay open to us the secrets of our own. ~ *William Hazlitt*

You know you've read a good book when you turn the last page and feel a little as if you have lost a friend. ~ *Paul Sweeney*

It is what you read when you don't have to that determines what you will be when you can't help it. ~ *Oscar Wilde*

Lord! When you sell a man a book you don't sell just twelve ounces of paper, ink and glue - you sell him a whole new life. Love and friendship and humor and ships at sea by night - there's all heaven and earth in a book, a real book. ~ *Christopher Morley*

I've never known any trouble that an hour's reading didn't assuage. ~ *Charles de Secondat*

Books are the bees which carry the quickening pollen from one mind to another. ~ *James Russell Lowell*

Books can be dangerous. The best ones should be labeled "This could change your life. ~ *Helen Exley*

There is a wonder in reading Braille that the sighted will never know: to touch words and have them touch you back. ~ *Jim Fiebig*

This will never be a civilized country until we expend more money for books than we do for chewing gum. ~ *Elbert Hubbard*

If you resist reading what you disagree with, how will you ever acquire deeper insights into what you believe? The things most worth reading are precisely those that challenge our convictions. ~ *Author Unknown*

When I get a little money, I buy books. If any is left, I buy food and clothes. ~ *Erasmus*

We don't need a list of rights and wrongs, tables of dos and don'ts: we need books, time, and silence. *Thou shalt not* is soon forgotten, but *Once upon a time* lasts forever. ~ *Philip Pullman*

Reading is the sole means by which we slip, involuntarily, often helplessly, into another's skin, another's voice, another's soul. ~ *Joyce Carol Oates*

Reputation

It takes 20 years to build a reputation and five minutes to ruin it. If you think about that you'll do things differently. ~ *Warren Buffett*

A good name is more desirable than great riches; to be esteemed is better than silver or gold. ~ *Proverbs 22:1*

Character is like a tree and reputation like its shadow. The shadow is what we think of it; the tree is the real thing. ~ *Abraham Lincoln*

Many a man's reputation would not know his character if they met on the street. ~ *Elbert Hubbard*

If you can't get rid of the skeleton in your closet, you'd best teach it to dance. ~ *William Shakespeare*

A brand for a company is like a reputation for a person. You earn reputation by trying to do hard things well. ~ *Jeff Bezos*

The reputation of a man is like his shadow, gigantic when it precedes him, and pigmy in its proportions when it follows. ~ *Alexandre De Talleyrand*

Respect

Treat others with respect and others will respect you. ~ *Unknown*

Good manners reflect something from inside, an innate sense of consideration for others and respect for yourself. ~ *Emily Post*

Good people don't have to throw dirt on others to feel better about themselves. ~ *Unknown*

Love and respect are the most important aspects of parenting and of all relationships. ~ *Jodie Foster*

You can't do whatever you want to people and expect to get away with it. ~ *Darcy Drake*

The best way to multiply respect is to share it with others ~ *Unknown*

Revenge

An eye for an eye can make the whole world blind. ~ *Unknown*

Revenge ... is like a rolling stone, which, when a man hath forced up a hill, will return upon him with a greater violence, and break those bones of the one whose force gave it motion. ~ *Albert Schweitzer*

There is no revenge so complete as forgiveness. ~ *Josh Billings*

Role Model

You've got to be careful whom you pattern yourself after because you're likely to become just like them. ~ *Rich Mayo*

If you as parents cut corners, your children will too. If you lie, they will too. If you spend all your money on yourselves and tithe no portion of it for charities, colleges, churches, synagogues, and civic causes, your children won't either. And if parents snicker at racial and gender jokes, another generation will pass on the poison adults still have not had the courage to snuff out. ~ *Marian Wright Edelman*

Role modeling is the most basic responsibility of parents. Parents are handing life's scripts to their children, scripts that in all likelihood will be acted out for the rest of the children s lives. ~ *Stephen R. Covey*

Each person must live their life as a model for others. ~ *Rosa Parks*

Don't worry that children never listen to you. Worry that they are always watching you. ~ *Robert Fulghum*

You are in charge of your feelings, beliefs, and actions. And you teach others how to behave toward you. While you cannot change other people, you can influence them through your own behaviors and actions. By being a living role model of what you want to receive from others, you create more of what you want in your life. ~ *Eric Allenbaugh*

You don't have to know people personally for them to be role models. Some of my most important role models were historical or literary figures that I only read about—never actually met. ~ *John Wilson*

The most important role models in people's lives, it seems, aren't superstars or household names. They're 'everyday' people who quietly set examples for you—coaches, teachers, and parents. People about whom you say to yourself, perhaps not even consciously, I want to be like that. ~ *Tim Foley*

S

Sacrifice

Dreams do come true, you can have anything in life if you are willing to sacrifice everything else for it. ~ *J.M. Barrie*

Sacrifice is part of life. It's supposed to be. It's not something to regret. It's something to aspire to. ~ *Mitch Alborn*

The only way to truly get more out of life for yourself is to give part of yourself away. ~ *Jim Stovall*

Determination is living a few years of your life like most people won't, so that you can spend the rest of your life like most people can't. ~ *Anonymous*

I hated every minute of training, but I said, don't quit. Suffer now and live the rest of your life as a champion. De termination rules! ~ *Mohammad Ali*

The ultimate test of man's conscience may be his willingness to sacrifice something today for future generations whose words of thanks will not be heard. ~ *Gaylord Nelson*

Great achievement is born of great sacrifice and is never the result of selfishness. ~ *Napoleon Hill*

Sales

Your will, Confidence and enthusiasm are the greatest sales producers in any kind of economy. ~ *O. B. Smith*

Don't sell your product or service, sell what the product or service can do. ~ *Ben Feldman*

If you are not taking care of your customer, your competitor will. ~ *Bob Hooey*

The key is not to call the decision maker. The key is to have the decision maker call you. ~ *Jeffrey Gitomer*

Timid salesmen have skinny kids. ~ *Zig Ziglar*

If you work just for money, you'll never make it. But if you love what you are doing, and always put the customer first, success will be yours. ~ *Ray Kroc*

To succeed in sales, simply talk to lots of people every day. And here's what's exciting – there are lots of people! ~ *Jim Rohn*

I do not think there is any other quality so essential to success of any kind as the quality of perseverance. It overcomes almost everything, even nature. ~ *John D. Rockefeller*

Sales are contingent upon the attitude of the salesman, not the attitude of the prospect. ~ *William Clement Stone*

The secret of man's success resides in his insight into the moods of people, and his tact in dealing with them. ~ *J. G. Holland*

How you think when you lose determines how long it will be until you win. ~ *Gilbert K. Chesterton*

A salesman, like the battery in your car, is constantly discharging energy. Unless he is recharged at frequent intervals he soon runs dry. This is one of the greatest responsibilities of sales leadership. ~ *R. H. Grant*

You don't close a sale, you open a relationship if you want to build a long-term, successful enterprise. ~ *Patricia Fripp*

The sale begins when the customer says yes. ~ *Harvey MacKay*

Everyone lives by selling something. ~ *Robert Louis Stevenson*

I have never worked a day in my life without selling. If I believe in something, I sell it, and I sell it hard. ~ *Estée Lauder*

A smart salesperson listens to emotions not facts. ~ *Unknown*

For every sale you miss because you're too enthusiastic, you will miss a hundred because you're not enthusiastic enough. ~ *Zig Ziglar*

There are going to be times when you can't make everyone happy. Don't expect to and you won't be disappointed. Just do your best for each client in each situation as it arises. Then, learn from each situation how to do it better the next time. ~ *Tom Hopkins*

Always be closing...That doesn't mean you're always closing the deal, but it does mean that you need to be always closing on the next step in the process. ~ *Shane Gibson*

It is not your customer's job to remember you. It is your obligation and responsibility to make sure they don't have the chance to forget you. ~ *Patricia Fripp*

The difference between a successful person and others is not a lack of strength, not a lack of knowledge, but rather a lack of will. ~ *Vince Lombardi*

The man who will use his skill and constructive imagination to see how much he can give for a dollar, instead of how little he can give for a dollar, is bound to succeed. ~ *Henry Ford*

The most unprofitable item ever manufactured is an excuse. ~ *John Mason*

Success is the culmination of failures, mistakes, false starts, confusion, and the determination to keep going anyway. ~ *Nick Gleason*

Most people think "selling" is the same as "talking". But the most effective salespeople know that listening is the most important part of their job. ~ *Roy Bartell*

The best sales questions have your expertise wrapped into them. ~ *Jill Konrath*

The questions you ask are more important than anything you could ever say. ~ *Tom Freese*

Excellence is not a skill. It's an attitude. ~ *Ralph Marston*

Try not to become a person of success but try to become a person of value. ~ *Albert Einstein*

Self-pity is an acid which eats holes in happiness. ~ *Earl Nightingale*

Your competition is EVERYTHING else your prospect could conceivably spend their money on. ~ *Don Cooper*

Prospecting - Find the man with the problem. ~ *Ben Friedman*

If opportunity doesn't knock, build a door. ~ *Milton Berle*

The way you position yourself at the beginning of a relationship has profound impact on where you end up. ~ *Ron Karr*

A good listener is not only popular everywhere, but after a while he knows something. ~ *Wilson Mizner*

Self-Esteem

Everyone is a genius. But if you judge a fish on its ability to climb a tree, it will live its whole life believing that it is stupid. ~ *Albert Einstein*

A bird sitting on a tree is never afraid of the branch breaking, because her trust is not on the branch but on her own wings. Always believe in yourself. ~ *Unknown*

An arrow can only be shot by pulling it backward, so when life is dragging you back with difficulties, it means that it's getting ready to launch you into something great. So just focus and keep aiming. ~ *Unknown*

Wanting to be someone else is a waste of the person you are. ~ *Marilyn Monroe*

Never be bullied into silence. Never allow yourself to be made a victim. Accept no one's definition of your life but instead, define yourself. ~ *Harvey Fierstein*

Don't let someone else's opinion of you become your reality. ~ *Les Brown*

When you're different, sometimes you don't see the millions of people who accept you for what you are. All you notice is the person who doesn't. ~ *Jodi Picoult*

As long as you look for someone else to validate who you are by seeking their approval, you are setting yourself up for disaster. You have to be whole and complete in yourself. No one can give you that. You have to know who you are - what others say is irrelevant. ~ *Nic Sheff*

How many of your goals and dreams have been aborted because of self-doubt? How much more are you capable of then you actually think? ~ *Talayah G. Stovall*

The worst loneliness is to not be comfortable with yourself. ~ *Mark Twain*

Why should we worry about what others think of us, do we have more confidence in their opinions than we do our own? ~ *Brigham Young*

You're always with yourself, so you might as well enjoy the company. ~ *Diane Von Furstenberg*

Everything that happens to you is a reflection of what you believe about yourself. We cannot outperform our level of self-esteem. We cannot draw to ourselves more than we think we are worth. ~ *Iyanla Vanzant*

Believe in yourself! Have faith in your abilities! Without a humble but reasonable confidence in your own powers you cannot be successful or happy. ~ *Norman Vincent Peale*

What you think about yourself is much more important than what others think of you. ~ *Marcus Annaeus Seneca*

How would your life be different if you stopped allowing other people to dilute or poison your day with their words or opinions? Let today be the day You stand strong in the truth of your beauty, and journey through your day without attachment to the validation of others - *Steve Maraboli*

Plant your own garden and decorate your own soul, instead of waiting for someone to bring you flowers. ~ *Veronica A. Shoffstall*

Make a personal decision to be in love with the most beautiful, exciting, worthy person ever, – you! ~ *Wayne Dyer*

If you aren't good at loving yourself, you will have a difficult time loving anyone, since you'll resent the time and energy you give another person that you aren't even giving to yourself. ~ *Barbara De Angelis*

To love oneself is the beginning of a life-long romance. ~ *Oscar Wilde*

With everything that has happened to you, you can either feel sorry for yourself, or treat what has happened as a gift. Everything is either an opportunity to grow or an obstacle to keep you from growing. You get to choose. ~ *Wayne Dyer*

Love is but the discovery of ourselves in others, and the delight in the recognition. ~ *Alexander Smith*

A loving person lives in a loving world. A hostile person lives in a hostile world. Everyone you meet is your mirror. ~ *Ken Keyes*

Sense of Humor

Anyone is automatically a lot more attractive when they are funny. ~ *Karen Hughes*

Through humor, you can soften some of the worst blows that life delivers. And once you find laughter, no matter how painful your situation might be, you can survive it. ~ *Unknown*

A sense of humor is needed armor. Joy in one's heart and some laughter on ones lips is a sign that the person down deep has a pretty good grasp of life. ~ *Hugh Sidey*

A good sense of humor is an escape valve for the pressures of life. ~ *Richard G. Scott*

Common sense and a sense of humor are the same thing, moving at different speeds. A sense of humor is just common sense, dancing. ~ *William James*

Good humor is a tonic for mind and body. It is the best antidote for anxiety and depression. It is a business asset. It attracts and keeps friends. It lightens human burdens. It is the direct route to serenity and contentment. ~ *Grenville Kleiser*

A well-developed sense of humor is the pole that adds balance to your steps as you walk the tightrope of life. ~ *William Arthur Ward*

Humor helps people who are oppressed to smile at the situation that pains them. ~ *Simon Wiesenthal*

I have seen what a laugh can do. It can transform almost unbearable tears into something bearable, even hopeful. ~ *Bob Hope*

Humor has bailed me out of more tight situations than I can think of. If you go with your instincts and keep your humor, creativity follows. With luck, success comes, too. ~ *Jimmy Buffett*

Anybody with a good sense of humor is one up on their competition. We respond to somebody who has the ability to make us laugh. It's a bonding influence. ~ *Robert Orben*

A keen sense of humor helps us to overlook the unbecoming, understand the unconventional, tolerate the unpleasant, overcome the unexpected, and outlast the unbearable. ~ *Billy Graham*

Servant

How wonderful it is that nobody need wait a single moment before starting to improve the world. ~ *Anne Frank*

Act as if what you do makes a difference. It does. ~ *William James*

Everyone thinks of changing the world, but no one thinks of changing himself. ~ *Leo Nikolaevich Tolstoy*

Being good is commendable, but only when it is combined with doing good is it useful. ~ *Author Unknown*

I am a little pencil in the hand of a writing God who is sending a love letter to the world. ~ *Mother Teresa*

I am only one, but I am one. I cannot do everything, but I can do something. And I will not let what I cannot do interfere with what I can do. ~ *Edward Everett Hale*

The willingness to share does not make one charitable; it makes one free. ~ *Robert Brault*

If you can't feed a hundred people, then feed just one. ~ *Mother Teresa*

Never worry about numbers. Help one person at a time, and always start with the person nearest you. ~ *Mother Teresa*

He who gives when he is asked has waited too long. ~ *Sunshine Magazine*

While earning your daily bread, be sure you share a slice with those less fortunate. ~ *H. Jackson Brown Jr.*

The difference between a helping hand and an outstretched palm is a twist of the wrist. ~ *Laurence Leamer*

No man stands so straight as when he stoops to help a boy. ~ *Knights of Pythagoras*

In about the same degree as you are helpful, you will be happy. ~ *Karl Reiland*

If you have no will to change it, you have no right to criticize it. ~ *Author Unknown*

When you dig another out of their troubles, you find a place to bury your own. ~ *Author Unknown*

Successful people are always looking for opportunities to help others. Unsuccessful people are always asking, what's in it for me? ~ *Brian Tracy*

Things of the spirit differ from things material in that the more you give the more you have. ~ *Christopher Morley*

Being a man or a woman is a matter of birth. Being a man or a woman who makes a difference is a matter of choice. ~ *Byron Garrett*

It's not that successful people are givers; it is that givers are successful people. ~ *Patti Thor*

Sorry

Sorry is a small word but it can bridge a huge gap, heal a terrible wound and repair any relationship. ~ *Unknown*

When you realize you've made a mistake, make amends immediately. It's easier to eat crow while it's still warm. ~ *Dan Heist*

There's one sad truth in life I've found, while journeying east and west -the only folks we really wound are those we love the best. We flatter those we scarcely know, we please the fleeting guest. And deal full many a thoughtless blow, to those who love us best. ~ *Ella Wheeler Wilcox*

An apology is a good way to have the last word. ~ *Unknown*

An apology is the superglue of life. It can repair just about anything. ~ *Lynn Johnston*

The only correct actions are those that demand no explanation and no apology. ~ *Red Auerbach*

Apology is a lovely perfume; it can transform the clumsiest moment into a gracious gift. ~ *Margaret Lee Runbeck*

If you were going to die soon and had only one phone call you could make, who would you call and what would you say? And why are you waiting? ~ *Stephen Levine*

For every minute you are angry, you lose sixty seconds of happiness. ~ *Unknown*

The most important trip you may take in life is meeting people halfway. ~ *Henry Boye*

Strategic Alliance

Companies should expand beyond their existing resources through licensing arrangements, strategic alliances, and supplier relationships. ~ *Business Week*

Alliances are an integral part of contemporary strategic thinking. ~ *Fortune Magazine*

The most beneficial type of partnering you can engage in is partnering with your customers. The benefits are compelling. You use it to gain customers, protect them from predation by competitors, and to protect your profit margins. ~ *Curtis E. Sahakian*

Businesses once grew by one of two ways; grass roots up, or by acquisition... Today they grow through alliances - all kinds of dangerous alliances. Joint ventures and customer partnerships which, by the way, very few people understand. ~ *Peter F. Drucker*

Since (with the use of partnerships) the organizations minimize the amount of internal change, you don't face the same resistance from reluctant managers and executives slowing you down as they protect their jobs, their egos or their turfs. This way you can avoid employee morale problems. ~ *Curtis E. Sahakian*

In regard to partnerships and alliances: At the end of the day, what really motivates people is the chance to really do something different - something that can't be done by either company individually - and to bring something of value to the market place. - Steve Steinhilber ~ *VP Strategic Alliances at Cisco*

The nature of innovation – the inherent definition of innovation – has changed today from what it was in the past. It's no longer individuals toiling in a laboratory, coming up with some great invention. It's not an individual. Its individuals. It's multidisciplinary. It's global. It's collaborative. ~ *Sam Palmisano - Chairman and CEO IBM Corporation*

There are three vital steps to partnering success: Determine what it is you need but don't have: customers, capital, special expertise, products, production capacity, or distribution channels. Second, determine who has what you need. And Three; Ask them for it, but, first make sure you have something they want or need. (This last point is the most important) ~ *Curtis E. Sahakian*

If you do not seek out allies and helpers, then you will be isolated and weak. ~ *Sun Tzu*

The forces of a powerful ally can be useful and good to those who have recourse to them... but are perilous to those who become dependent on them. ~ *Niccolo Machiavelli*

Joint Ventures, Alliances, and other Corporate Partnering's are fueling the growth of the world's most successful companies. The demand to deliver more new products, more quickly, and at lower prices has never been greater. Joint Ventures and other collaborative business arrangements are revolutionizing how winning companies compete. They permit companies to enter new markets and field new products that they otherwise couldn't do on their own. They are the quickest way to grow your company, particularly in times of change. ~ *Curtis E. Sahakian*

Strategy for Business

Strategic thinking is like showering, you have to keep doing it. ~ *Olan Hendrix*

Victorious warriors win first and then go to war, while defeated warriors go to war first and then seek to win. ~ *Sun Tzu*

The essence of strategy is choosing what not to do. ~ *Michael E. Porter*

However beautiful the strategy, you should occasionally look at the results. ~ *Winston Churchill*

The aim of marketing is to know and understand the customer so well the product or service fits him and sells itself. ~ *Peter Drucker*

Sound strategy starts with having the right goal. ~ *Michael Porter*

Strategy without tactics is the slowest route to victory. Tactics without strategy is the noise before defeat. ~ *Sun Tzu*

Your purpose explains what you are doing with your life. Your vision explains how you are living your purpose. Your goals enable you to realize your vision. ~ *Bob Proctor*

In marketing I've seen only one strategy that can't miss - and that is to market to your best customers first, your best prospects second and the rest of the world last. ~ *John Romero*

What do you want to achieve or avoid? The answers to this question are objectives. How will you go about achieving your desire results? The answer to this you can call strategy. ~ *William E. Rothschild*

What business strategy is all about, what distinguishes it from all other kinds of business planning is, in a word, competitive advantage. Without competitors there would be no need for strategy, for the sole purpose of strategic planning is to enable the company to gain, as efficiently as possible, a sustainable edge over its competitors. ~ *Kenichi Ohmae*

If you can't describe your strategy in twenty minutes, simply and in plain language, you haven't got a plan. But, people may say, "I've got a complex strategy". It can't be reduced to a page. That's nonsense. That's not a complex strategy. It's a complex thought about the strategy. ~ *Larry Bossidy,*

The expert in battle seeks his victory from strategic advantage and does not demand it from his men. ~ *Sun Tzu*

The Company without a strategy is willing to try anything. ~ *Michael Porter*

In real life, strategy is actually very straightforward. You pick a general direction and implement like hell. ~ *Jack Welch*

Success

Success is the ability to go from failure to failure without losing your enthusiasm. ~ *Winston Churchill*

To be successful in life you need 3 bones. A wishbone, a backbone and funny bone. ~ *Reba McEntire*

Identify your problems but give your power and energy to solutions. ~ *Tony Robbins*

You live longer once you realize that any time spent being unhappy is wasted. ~ *Ruth E. Renkl*

Things work out best for those who make the best of how things work out. ~ *John Wooden*

Let no feeling of discouragement prey upon you, and in the end you are sure to succeed. ~ *Abraham Lincoln*

If you are not willing to risk the usual, you will have to settle for the ordinary. ~ *Jim Rohn*

Improve your business, your life, your relationships, your finances and your health. When you do the whole world improves. ~ *Mark Victor Hansen*

Wanting something is not enough. You must hunger for it. Your motivation must be absolutely compelling in order to overcome the obstacles that will invariably come your way. ~ Les Brown

Be content to act and leave the talking to others. ~ *Baltasa*

The more you lose yourself in something bigger than yourself, the more energy you will have. ~ *Norman Vincent Peale*

The way we dress affects the way we think, the way we feel, the way we act, and the way others react to us. ~ *Judith Rasband*

Your clothes should be tight enough to show you're a woman, but loose enough to show you're a lady. ~ *Marilyn Monroe*

Be a first-rate version of yourself, not a second rate version of someone else. ~ *Emily Post*

Dress shabbily and they remember the dress, dress impeccably and they remember the woman. ~ *Coco Chenel*

You want it, you see it, you believe it, you pursue it, you do it, you own it, and it's yours! ~ *Joseph Murphy*

Be willing to go out on limb - that is where the fruit is. ~ *H. Jackson Browne*

Too many of us are not living our dreams because we are living our fears. ~ *Les Brown*

As long as you're going to be thinking anyway, think big. ~ *Donald Trump*

Opportunity is missed by most people because it is dressed in overalls and looks like work. ~ *Thomas Edison*

The only place where success comes before work is in the dictionary. ~ *Vidal Sassoon*

Capital isn't scarce; vision is. ~ *Sam Walton*

Failure defeats losers, failure inspires winners. ~ *Robert T. Kiyosaki*

Some people dream of great accomplishments, while others stay awake and do them. ~ *Anonymous*

Going into business for yourself, becoming an entrepreneur, is the modern-day equivalent of pioneering on the old frontier. ~ *Paula Nelson*

Poor people have a big TV. Rich people have big library. ~ *Jim Rohn*

A goal is a dream with a deadline. ~ *Napoleon Hill*

Every day I get up and look through the Forbes list of the richest people in America. If I'm not there, I go to work. ~ *Vinnie Rege*

Expect the best. Prepare for the worst. Capitalize on what comes. ~ *Zig Ziglar*

The best reason to start an organization is to make meaning; to create a product or service to make the world a better place. ~ *Guy Kawasaki*

A friendship founded on business is a good deal better than a business founded on friendship. ~ *John D. Rockefeller*

Logic will get you from A to B. Imagination will take you everywhere. ~ *Albert Einstein*

Success is liking yourself, liking what you do, and liking how you do it. ~ *Maya Angelou*

Without continual growth and progress, such words as improvement, achievement, and success have no meaning. ~ *Benjamin Franklin*

Big pay and little responsibility are circumstances seldom found together. ~ *Napoleon Hill*

T

Teaching

Treat people as if they were what they ought to be and you help them become what they are capable of becoming. ~ *Goethe*

The authority of those who teach is very often a hindrance to those who wish to learn. ~ *Cicero*

Learning is finding out what we already know. Doing is demonstrating that you know it. Teaching is reminding others that they know just as well as you. You are all learners, doers, and teachers. ~ *Richard Bach*

A teacher who is attempting to teach without inspiring the pupil with a desire to learn is hammering on cold iron. ~ *Horace Mann*

The great end of education is to discipline rather than to furnish the mind; to train it to the use of its own powers rather than to fill it with the accumulation of others. ~ *Tyron Edwards*

A hundred years from now, it will not matter what kind of car I drove, what kind of house I lived in, how much money I had in the bank...but that the world may be a better place because I made a difference in the life of a child. ~ *Forest Witcraft*

The job of an educator is to teach students to see the vitality in themselves. ~ *Joseph Campbell*

Education is not to reform students or amuse them or to make them expert technicians. It is to unsettle their minds, widen their horizons, inflame their intellects, and teach them to think straight, if possible. ~ *Robert M. Hutchins*

It is important that students bring a certain ragamuffin, barefoot irreverence to their studies; they are not here to worship what is known, but to question it. ~ *Jacob Bronowski*

Teaching kids to count is fine but teaching them what counts is best. ~ *Bob Talber*

Tell me and I forget. Teach me and I remember. Involve me and I learn. ~ *Benjamin Franklin*

Do not train a child to learn by force or harshness; but direct them to it by what amuses their minds, so that you may be better able to discover with accuracy the peculiar bent of the genius of each. ~ *Plato*

Everybody is a genius. But if you judge a fish by its ability to climb a tree it will live its whole life believing that it is stupid. ~ *Anonymous*

They may forget what you said but they will never forget how you made them feel. ~ *Carol Buchner*

It is not what is poured into a student that counts but what is planted. ~ *Linda Conway*

It is the supreme art of the teacher to awaken joy in creative expression and knowledge. ~ *Albert Einstein*

If a child is to keep alive his inborn sense of wonder, he needs the companionship of at least one adult who can share it, rediscovering with him the joy, the excitement, and the mystery of the world we live in. ~ *Rachel Carlson*

We learn by example and by direct experience because there are real limits to the adequacy of verbal instruction. ~ *Malcom Gladwell*

The greatest sign of success for a teacher is to be able to say, the children are now working as if I did not exist. ~ *Maria Montessori*

Good teaching is more a giving of right questions than a giving of right answers. ~ *Josef Albers*

Team Work

Teamwork makes the dream work. ~ *John Maxwell*

I am a member of a team, and I rely on the team, I defer to it and sacrifice for it, because the team, not the individual, is the ultimate champion. ~ *Mia Hamm*

A snowflake is one of God's most fragile creations but look what they can do when they stick together! ~ *Author Unknown*

Team members felt strong and capable because their input made a difference. Support others, and they are more likely to support you. ~ *Marianne Hane*

None of us has gotten where we are soley by pulling ourselves up by own bootstraps. We got here because somebody bent down to help us. ~ *Unknown*

Cooperation is the thorough conviction that nobody can get there unless everybody gets there. ~ *Virginia Burden*

Sticks in a bundle are unbreakable. ~ *Kenyan Proverb*

You need to be aware of what others are doing, applaud their efforts, acknowledge their successes, and encourage them in their pursuits. When we all help one another, everybody wins. ~ *Jim Stovall (Creator of "The Lamp" movie)*

Coming together is a beginning. Keeping together is progress. Working together is success. ~ *Henry Ford*

None of us is as smart as all of us. ~ *Ken Blanchard*

A man may do an immense deal of good, if he does not care who gets the credit for it. - *Father Strickland*

Teamwork is the ability to work together toward a common vision. The ability to direct individual accomplishment toward organizational objectives. It is the fuel that allows common -

people to attain uncommon results. ~ *Andrew Carnegie*

A chain is only as strong as its weakest link. ~ *Author Unknown*

If everyone is moving forward together, then success takes care of itself. ~ *Henry Ford*

The ratio of "We's to I's" is the best indicator of the development of a team. ~ *Lewis B. Ergen*

Thinking

Thoughts become words, words become actions, actions develop habits, habits develop your character and character will determine your destiny ~ *James Allen*

One of the reasons people don't achieve their dreams is that they desire to change their results without changing their thinking. ~ *John Maxwell*

Big thinkers are specialists in creating positive, forward-thinking, optimistic pictures in their own minds and in the minds of others. ~ *David Schwartz*

Remember just like water takes the shape of the pipe it flows through, the life principle in you flows through you according to the nature of your thoughts. ~ *Joseph Murphy*

An optimist looks at a glass and says the glass is half full. A pessimist looks at a glass and says the glass is half empty. An engineer looks at a glass and says, that glass is twice as big as it needs to be. ~ *Unknown*

Here's the problem. Most people are thinking about what they don't want, and they're wondering why it shows up over and over again. ~ *John Assaraf*

Thoughts become things. If you see it in your mind, you will hold it in your hand. ~ *Bob Proctor*

One of the keys to maximizing realistic thinking is aligning your resources with your objectives. ~ *John Maxwell*

Actions always have consequences; realistic thinking helps determine what those consequences will be. ~ *Unknown*

Keep your mind off the things you don't want, by keeping it on the things you do want. ~ *W. Clement Stone*

You have to think about big things while you're doing small things, so that all the small things go in the right direction. ~ *Alvin Toffler*

Where success is concerned, people are not measured in inches, or pounds, or college degrees, or family background; they are measured by the size of their thinking. ~ *David Schwartz*

You will find throughout all of nature, the law of action and reaction, rest and motion. These two must balance and then there will be harmony and equilibrium. You are here to let the life principle flow through you rhythmically and harmoniously. The intake and the outgo must be equal, the impression and the expression must be equal. All of your frustration is due to unfulfilled desire. ~ *Joseph Murphy*

If you want to be a sharp thinker, be around sharp people. ~ *Unknown*

Do you want to know what you think about most of the time? Take a look at the results you're getting. That will tell you exactly what's going on inside. ~ *Bob proctor*

Learning to write is learning to think. You don't know anything clearly unless you can state it in writing. ~ *S.L. Hayakawa*

For the flower to blossom, you need the right soil as well as the right seed. The same is true to cultivate good thinking. ~ *William Bernbach*

Time Management

Until you value yourself, you won't value your time. Until you value your time, you will not do anything with it. ~ *M. Scott Peck*

Yesterday is a canceled check, Tomorrow's a promissory note, today is cash in hand and it's the only cash you have so spend it wisely. ~ *Kim Lyons*

I don't have time, is the grown-up version of, the dog ate my homework. ~ *Anonymous*

Don't wait. The time will never be just right. ~ *Napoleon Hill*

The only reason for time is so that everything doesn't happen at once. ~ *Albert Einstein*

Think ahead. Don't let day-to-day operations drive out planning. ~ *Donald Rumsfeld*

Planning is bringing the future into the present so that you can do something about it now. ~ *Alan Lakein*

Trust

Trust is the emotional glue that binds followers and leaders together. ~ *Warren Bennis*

Trust takes years to build, seconds to break and forever to repair. ~ *Unknown*

Few things help an individual more than to place responsibility upon him and to let him know that you trust him. ~ *Booker T. Washington*

The best way to find out if you can trust somebody is to trust them. ~ *Ernest Hemingway*

Trust is letting go of needing to know all the details before you open your heart. ~ *Unknown*

Show me a man who cannot be trusted to do little things and I'll show you a man who cannot be trusted to do big things. ~ *Laurence D Bell*

If you give your trust to a person who does not deserve it, you actually give him the power to destroy you. ~ *Unknown*

You must begin to trust yourself. If you do not then you will forever be looking to others to prove your own merit to you, and you will never be satisfied. You will always be asking others what to do, and at the same time, resenting those from whom you seek such aid. ~ *Jane Roberts*

Trust is like an eraser, it gets smaller and smaller after every mistake. ~ *Unknown*

A relationship without trust is like a car without gas, you can stay in it as long as you want but it won't go anywhere. ~ *Unknown*

V

Values

Good values are easier caught than taught. ~ *Zig Ziglar*

Living in a way that reflects one's values is not just about what you do, it is also about how you do things. ~ *Deborah Day*

To feel more fulfilled your actions and activities need to be in alignment with what you deem important. ~ *Deborah Day*

Your life is your statement to the world representing your values, your beliefs, your dreams. ~ *David Arenson*

When your values are clear to you, making decisions becomes easier. ~ *Roy Disney*

Every one of us receives and passes on an inheritance. The inheritance may not be an accumulation of earthly possessions or acquired riches, but whether we realize it or not, our choices, words, actions, and values will impact someone and form the heritage we hand down. ~ *Ben Hardesty*

Vision

If you do not see yourself as a winner, you cannot perform as a winner. ~ *Zig Ziglar*

You must understand that seeing is believing, but also know that believing is seeing. ~ *Dennis Waitley*

173

People will never attain what they cannot see themselves doing. ~ *Karen Ford*

Whatever you can do or dream you can, begin it. Boldness has genius, and magic and power in it. Begin it now. ~ *Goethe*

The greatest danger for most of us is not that our aim is too high, and we miss it, but that it is too low and we reach it. ~ *Michelangelo*

Your vision will become clear only when you look into your heart. He who looks outside, dreams. He who looks inside awakens. ~ *Carl Jung*

The empires of the future are empires of the mind. ~ *Winston Churchill*

Vision without action is a daydream. Action with without vision is a nightmare. ~ *Japanese Proverb*

Where there is no vision the people perish. ~ *Proverbs 29:18*

Vision without execution is hallucination. ~ *Thomas Edison*

If you limit your choices only to what seems possible or reasonable, you disconnect yourself from what you truly want, and all that is left is a compromise. ~ *Robert Fritz*

Cherish your visions and your dreams as they are the children of your soul, the blueprints of your ultimate achievements. ~ *Napoleon Hill*

Vision animates, inspires, and transforms purpose into action. ~ *Warren Bennis*

W

Wealth

The person who doesn't know where his next dollar is coming from usually doesn't know where his last dollar went. ~ *Unknown*

Money is good for nothing unless you know the value of it by experience. ~ *P.T Barnum*

Empty pockets never held anyone back. Only empty heads and empty hearts can do that. ~ *Norman Vincent Peale*

If you want to know what a man is really like, take notice of how he acts when he loses money. ~ *Simone Weil*

You can only become truly accomplished at something you love. Don't make money your goal. Instead, pursue the things you love doing, and then do them so well that people can't take their eyes off you. ~ *Maya Angelou*

Don't tell me where your priorities are. Show me where you spend your money and I'll tell you what they are. ~ *James W. Frick*

Buy when everyone else is selling and hold until everyone else is buying. That's not just a catchy slogan. It's the very essence of successful investing. ~ *J. Paul Getty*

If you have a family who loves you and you have great health, you're richer than you think. ~ *Mary Angeline Gleed*

If money is your hope for independence you will never have it. The only real security that a man will have in this world is a reserve of knowledge, experience, and ability. ~ *Henry Ford*

The safe way to double your money is to fold it over once and put it in your pocket. ~ *Frank Hubbard*

I would rather have one percent of a hundred people efforts than one hundred percent of my own. ~ *J Paul Getty*

Never spend your money before you have it. ~ *Thomas Jefferson*

There is a very easy way to return from a casino with a small fortune, go there with a large one. ~ *Jack Yelton*

My problem lies in reconciling my gross habits with my net income. - *Errol Flynn*

Car sickness is the feeling you get when the monthly payment is due. ~ *Author Unknown*

The real measure of your wealth is how much you'd be worth if you lost all your money. ~ *Author Unknown*

The only reason a great many American families don't own an elephant is that they have never been offered an elephant for a dollar down and easy weekly payments. ~ *Mad Magazine*

Business is the art of extracting money from another man's pocket without resorting to violence. ~ *Max Amsterdam*

Winning

If a tie is like kissing your sister than losing is like kissing your grandmother with her teeth out. ~ *George Brett*

Second place is just the first loser. ~ *Dale Earnhardt*

Winning doesn't always mean being first, winning means you're doing better than you've done before. ~ *Unknown*

Things wasted, whether our food or our gigts and talents, can never be regained. What gifts and talents are you storing in the "freezer" of your life that you haven't thawed out in a while? ~ *Talayah G. Stovall*

Winning means you're willing to go longer, work harder and give more than anyone else. ~ *Vince Lombardi*

The difference in winning and losing is most often not quitting. ~ *Walt Disney*

Talent wins games, but teamwork and intelligence wins championships. ~ *Michael Jordan*

Winners make a habit of manufacturing their own positive expectations in advance of the event. ~ *Brian Tracy*

You were born to win, but to be a winner you must plan to win, prepare to win and expect to win. ~ *Zig Ziglar*

Winning is a state of mind that embraces everything you do. ~ *Bryce Courtenay*

Obstacles are challenges for winners and excuses for losers. ~ *M.E Kerr*

Games are lost and won in your mind as much as they are on the field. ~ *Carl Deuker*

Win without boasting. Lose without excuse. ~ *Albert Payson Terhune*

I've missed more than 9000 shots in my career. I've lost almost 300 games. 26 times, I've been trusted to take the game winning shot and missed. I've failed over and over and over again in my life. And that is why I succeed. ~ *Michael Jordan*

Word Power

Mother Teresa understood the power of words. When she was invited to an ant-war rally, her response was "no", but if you ever decide to host a pro-peace rally, I will be there. ~ *The Secret*

The limits of your vocabulary and your ability to use them are also the limits of your world. ~ *Unknown*

When words are scarce they are seldom spent in vain. ~ *William Shakespeare, Richard II*

One great use of words is to hide our thoughts. ~ *Voltaire*

So difficult it is to show the various meanings and imperfections of words when we have nothing else but words to do it with. ~ *John Locke*

The great enemy of clear language is insincerity. When there is a gap between one's real and one's declared aims, one turns, as it were, instinctively to long words and exhausted idioms, like a cuttlefish squirting out ink. ~ *George Orwell*

We are masters of the unsaid words, but slaves of those we let slip out. ~ *Winston Churchill*

A vocabulary of truth and simplicity will be of service throughout your life. ~ *Winston Churchill*

The more the words, the less the meaning, and how does that profit anyone? ~ *Ecclesiastes 6:11*

The right word may be effective, but no word was ever as effective as a rightly timed pause. ~ *Mark Twain*

Words are so innocent and powerless as they are standing in a dictionary, how potent for good and evil they become in the hands of one who knows how to combine them. ~ *Nathaniel Hawthorne*

You can change your world by changing your words… Remember, death and life are in the power of the tongue. ~ *Joel Osteen*

Think twice before you speak, because your words and influence will plant the seed of either success or failure in the mind of another. ~ *Napoleon Hill*

Words do two major things: They provide food for the mind and create light for understanding and awareness. ~ *Jim Rohn*

Words are but the vague shadows of what we mean. Little audible links, they are, chaining together great inaudible feelings and purposes. ~ *Theodore Dreiser*

Kind words do not cost much. They never blister the tongue or lips. They make other people good-natured. They also produce their own image on the souls of man, and a beautiful image it is. ~ *Blaise Pascal*

Eating words has never given me indigestion ~ *Winston Churchill*

The difference between the almost right word & the right word is really a large matter—it's the difference between the lightning bug and the lightning. ~ *Mark Twain*

If you wouldn't write it and sign it, don't say it. ~ *Earl Wilson*

Speak clearly, if you speak at all; carve every word before you let it fall. ~ *Oliver Wendell Holmes*

It is with words as with sunbeams, the more they are condensed, the deeper they burn. ~ *Robert Southey*

When you have spoken the word, it reigns over you. When it is unspoken you reign over it. ~ *Proverb*

In words are seen the state of mind and character and disposition of the speaker. ~ *Plutarch*

But I tell you that men will have to give account on the Day of Judgment for every careless word they have spoken. For by your words you will be acquitted, and by your words you will be condemned. ~ *Matthew 12:36-38*

Among my most prized possessions are words that I have never spoken. ~ *Orson Rega Card*

He that uses too many words for explaining any subject doth, like the cuttlefish, hide himself for the most part in his own ink. ~ *John Ray*

There are thousands of thoughts lying within a man that he does not know till he takes up the pen and writes. ~ *William Thackeray*

There's a great power in words, if you don't hitch too many of them together. ~ *Josh Billings*

Don't, Sir, accustom yourself to use big words for little matters. ~ *Dr. Samuel Johnson*

Words, words, words! They shut one off from the universe. Three quarters of the time one's never in contact with things, only with the beastly words that stand for them. ~ *Aldous Huxley*

A torn jacket is soon mended; but hard words bruise the heart of a child. ~ *Henry Wadsworth Longfellow*

Worry

Worrying is like being on a treadmill, it keeps you occupied but you're not really going anywhere. ~ *Angel Gleed*

Worry does not empty tomorrow of its sorrow, it empties today of its strength. ~ *Leo Buscaglia*

If a problem is fixable, if a situation is such that you can do something about it, then there is no need to worry. If it's not fixable, then there is no help in worrying. There is no benefit in worrying whatsoever. ~ *His Holiness the Dalai Lama*

Do not anticipate trouble or worry about what may never happen. Keep in the sunlight. ~ *Benjamin Franklin*

Worry is a misuse of the imagination. ~ *Dan Zadra*

You can't wring your hands and roll up your sleeves at the same time. ~ *Pat Schroeder*

Worry is a means of using up the present moment in being consumed about something in the future, over which you have no control. ~ *Wayne Dyer*

My life has been full of terrible misfortunes most of which never happened. ~ *Michel de Montaigne*

BONUS SECTION

SUCCESS STRATEGIES

A SNEAK PEEK AT MY NEXT BOOK

12

These twelve proven, time tested, top success secrets of millionaire minds, are success strategies capable of supercharging your life and your business. And for the first time ever published, my amazing formula for solving any problem and building any dream.

Success is great but without significance it leaves you feeling empty. Only significance can give you fulfillment. Success is when you fill your own cup. Significance is when you fill the cups of others. The following master keys to success will help you do both.

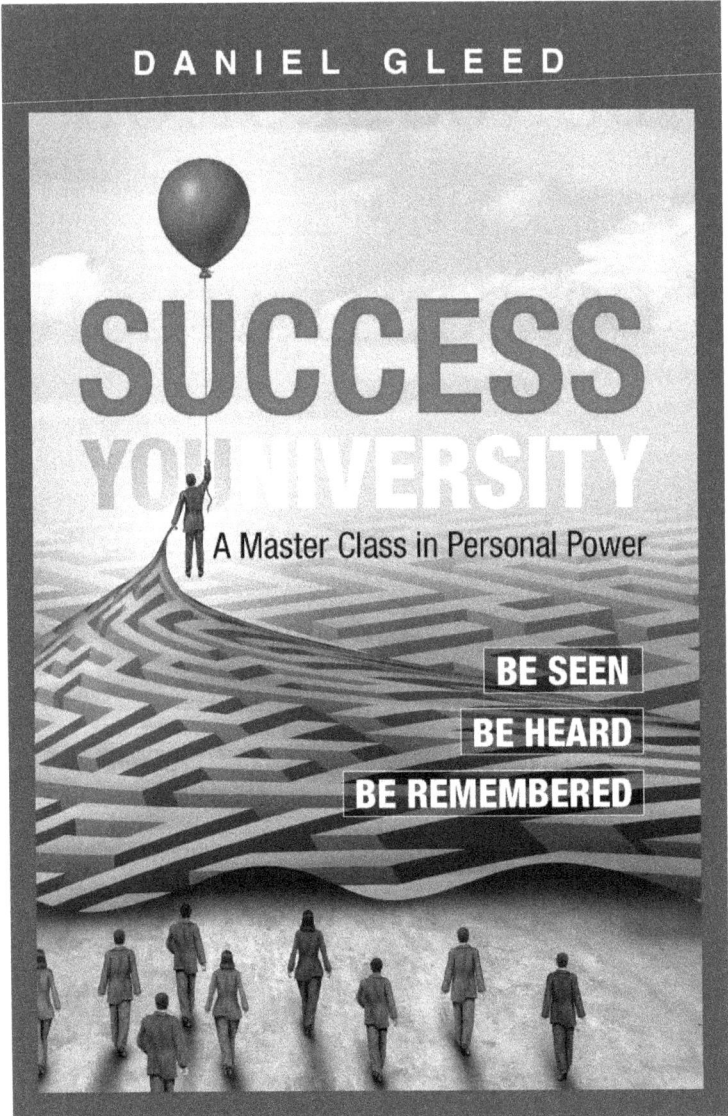

DANIEL GLEED

SUCCESS YOUNIVERSITY

A Master Class in Personal Power

BE SEEN
BE HEARD
BE REMEMBERED

Copyright 2018

The following content is a sneak peek at my new book. This book is loaded with brand new, never been seen before, ground breaking, future defining success strategies. The following is a very small taste of what you're going to see in the full book.

Enjoy these free bonus success strategies. Any one of them will lift you to new heights of success in business and in life, if you learn, apply and integrate them.

1

Lacuna Substrata

How to intentionally influence positive effects

Lacuna Substrata, not to be confused with Hakuna Matata, is a formula that can be applied in all areas of your life. Personal development, professional development, Spiritual development, relationships, health, hobbies and any situation that you will face in your life time.

To influence the outcome of any situation you must learn to control three things. I refer to these triplets as **the trio of majesty**. You must learn to control:

1. Your behavior
2. Your thoughts
3. Your visual imagery

Now, let me drill down a little deeper into each one of these for you.

1. **Your behavior** – This includes your actions and you're attitudes. You've heard the adage, it's not what you say,

it's how you say it. You can also say, it's not what you do, it's how you do it, and the attitude you choose to combine with it. In this case, it's all the above. Boil it down to 3 points, your actions, the things you say, and how you say them.

2. **Your thoughts** – this includes your internal dialog and your beliefs. What many call your self-talk. In this case we are concerned with self-talk at both the conscious level and the subconscious level.

3. **Your visual imagery** – meaning the pictures or images you repeatedly see or imagine inside your mind. These can be images or visual constructs of the way you see things in the present moment, or the way you see them in the subsequent, forthcoming continuation of your life in the future.

Learning to control these collectively is how you become a MOFO. And MOFO is an acronym for **M**aster **o**f **Fu**ture **O**utcomes and Effects.

BUT HOW DO YOU CONTROL ALL THESE THINGS?

- I can teach you a simple formula that is rich with wisdom, that will lift your ability to control the outcome of any situation.
- It will super charge your emotional intelligence.
- And make all your business and personal relationships sparkle and shine more than ever.

HERE IS MY MAGICAL FORMULA

The name of the formula is Lacuna Substrata. The formula goes as follows. "$S + R2 = E$"

Let Me Break It Down for You.

184

S stands for *situation*, this is any situation you face in life + **R2,** meaning your *response* or your *reaction* to the situation, equals, **E,** which is the effect on your life and potentially others as well.

The word *SPREE* will help you remember the formula. *Situation Plus Response Equals Effect.*

Situations in Your Life + How You Respond or React = The Effect.

WHAT IS A SITUATION?

A situation is created when two or more circumstances converge and become entangled, resulting in an outcome or an effect.

THE BOBBER AND THE HOOK

The bobber is used when fishing, it floats on the surface of the water. Attached to the bobber is a long piece of fishing line that extends beneath the surface and is attached to a hook. The hook is baited, and when a fish starts to nibble on the bait, the bobber floating on top of the water begins to move.

The bobber is the indicator that lets you know there is something going on beneath the surface. Many times, in life or in business, people will perceive a situation to be like the bobber, when there is really something more going on at the hook level.

They think the situation is the problem when the truth is, that the situation is the only the bobber. The situation is the indicator that something is going on beneath the surface and if you take the time to look beneath the surface you will discover the *circumstances* that have already created or are in the process of creating the situation. The metaphor of the bobber and the hook is a reminder that you may need to divide the circumstances from the situation and break them down, so you can take a closer look.

Most of the human population will blame the bobber (surface issue) unaware, or choosing to ignore the bigger problem, or problems going on at the hook level (beneath the surface).

You can choose to spend the rest of your life living on the surface, but you will never experience fulfillment, or what I call *ful-feel-ment*. *I call it ful-feel-ment* because fulfillment is a centered, peaceful *feeling* that your meant to be *full of*.

SUBSTRATA

The meaning of SUBSTRATA is: An underlying layer, or substance. The basis of something. (This is the hook level, where circumstances are lurking and many times have been buried, hiding behind the mask of a situation)

S/C *or* S Divided by C = Any **situation** divided by its **circumstances.**

One common mistake people make is responding to the bobber, meaning the *situation* as-a whole. Remember, a situation can only be created when two or more circumstances converge and become entangled. If a situation can only exist when two or more circumstances converge, then it makes sense that sometimes it is necessary to break the situation down and separate the circumstances that created it, *because one or more of the circumstances may require a different response.*

R2 EQUALS YOUR RESPONSE OR YOUR REACTION

Think of Response or Reaction Like Medicine

- If the patient is responding to the medication, that is a good thing, right? And if the patient is reacting to the medicine, that is a bad thing.

- In-regards to this formula and how it applies to your life, if you respond, you are in control, and that's a good thing.
- If you react, you are out of control. You are being controlled by the patterns of behavior that have been conditioned at the subconscious level. That is a bad thing in terms or reacting.

IT ALSO HELPS ME TO THINK OF R2D2

The R2 reminds me of the words *react or respond*. It also reminds me that the decision to react or respond is something I take complete ownership of. If I react then I have nobody to blame but myself for my actions.

The D2 reminds of the words *destroy or develop*. If I react, I'm delaying or destroying the possibility of a positive outcome or effect. If I respond, I'm in control of my attitude and my potential influence and I'm leaning toward developing a positive outcome or effect.

THERE IS A HIDDEN SECRET TO THIS FORMULA

When we **react** to a situation, it's happening on auto-pilot. Our thinking programs and behavioral patterns are running at the subconscious level on auto-pilot.

Now, you might be thinking, if all my reactions are generated by the programs and patterns that are running on autopilot, then how is this formula going to help me **respond** *rather than react?*

THE KEY TO UNLOCKING THE POWER OF THIS FORMULA IS HIDDEN IN PLAIN SIGHT. – CAN YOU SEE IT? ... S+R2 = E

My Dad and Mom use to tell me to engage my brain before I engage my lips, they would tell me to think before I speak. But that is easier said than done if things are running on autopilot. How do I stop and think?

There is something called "*pattern interrupt*" meaning if you can interrupt your pattern of thought, you'll be able to step into the magical place where you can think before you act. *Are you ready for the secret?*

LACUNA IS THE MAGIC OF THIS FORMULA

The meaning of LACUNA: *An unfilled SPACE*

Between any situation and your **reaction** or your **response** is a **space**, and inside that space is your freedom and power to interrupt programs and patterns. In the magical space lives your ability to take control of the three most powerful things in your life. Your behaviors, your thoughts and the images you hold in your mind. When you enter the space, and take control, you have the power to choose responses that intentionally influence positive outcomes and effects in any situation.

By the way, this magical place is also the place where all major success happens, it's where great leaders are made and it's the place where great ideas are discovered, it's where high achievers are created and it's the place where every millionaire has been made. It's the place where you can shape your future and control your destiny. In this space, you have the ability to live the life of your dreams.

The space is the magical place, and It will help you to think of the word **space** as an acronym for ...

Stop
Pause
And
Consider
Effect

BUT HOW DO I INTERRUPT THE PATTERN AND GET INTO THE SPACE

I use 3 words as a reminder to acknowledge the space. The three words that form my trigger phrase has also become my mantra for this formula and the mantra is, *Space Invaders Rule!!!*

When I find myself in a position where I need to interrupt a pattern, I say out loud or under my breath, *space invaders rule*. This brings the importance of the *space* fully into my awareness. This reminds me of the literal **space** that I need to enter mentally, emotionally and spiritually, as well as what I need to do inside the *space* which is to **S**top **P**ause **A**nd **C**onsider **E**ffect.

It causes me to turn my attention inward and listen to my breathing. This helps bring myself back to center and enter the space. Once I'm in the space I know that I have to evaluate 3 things. My behavior, my thoughts and my images, as they pertain to the current situation. And ask myself one important question.

what changes to my behavior, thoughts and images do I need to make in order to create the response that will produce the outcome or effect I'm looking for?

One last tip: I sometimes where a rubber band around my wrist and when a tense situation arises I will snap the rubber band against the skin on my wrist and then say to myself, *space invaders rule*, to interrupt the pattern and bring myself back to center which is where the space is located.

The space is the inward place where you can tap into your power to evaluate and make new and different choices and decisions. What I mean by that is, the best way to assess your out-look is to have an in-look. Turn your attention inward and self-evaluate. If there are other people involved in the situation, imagine yourself in their shoes. And last but-not least, always remember that you don't know what you don't know. There is always more to any situation than you know.

1. Interrupt the pattern – Say, *Space Invaders Rule* or snap the rubber band on your wrist, or both. (or make up your own technique)
2. Bring yourself back to center. Turn your attention inward and listen to your breathing.
3. Self-Evaluate – Submerse yourself into the space and evaluate your thoughts and the images in your mind. And consider the outcomes or effects of your possible responses or reactions. Spend as much time as you need to in the space to make the best choices and decisions.

One final gold nugget is, *everything matters*! This is another one of my mantras, because in both business and in life, *everything matters*. Everything you say, everything you don't say, everything you do and everything you don't do. Everything you think and everything you don't think, everything you feel and everything you don't feel. Everything produces an effect.

2

The Power of One

Own Your Position in Life

Total responsibility strengthens your power and your possibility. Your current position in life is the culmination of your past choices, decisions and experiences. It's a combination of the situations that have taken place in your life and how you have responded or reacted to them. In other words, you are living in the residual of your past choices and decisions, and they were based on your way of thinking.

If you are perfectly happy with all areas of your life and you feel there is no room for improvement than here is my advice. Enjoy those rose-colored glasses your wearing. Because the minute you take them off you will realize that there is *always* room for improvement. Human potential is unlimited, that's why there is always more room to grow, and that room is waiting to be realized and occupied by you.

Taking time to reflect periodically is always a great way to identify areas of opportunity for personal and professional growth. It's during reflection that our inner voice can be heard loud and clear as it tells us about a void that needs to be filled. Maybe it's an area of life that needs mending or a desire to try something different or learn something new. Life is constantly in flux, that is why it's called a journey, and along the way, from time to time we are presented with gaps in our lives. Gaps come in various sizes and they can be found at work or at home. Challenges can, and will present themselves in finances, relationships, spirituality or any other area of life and when they do, they can create a gap.

In Taking Responsibility for Helping to Create the Gap, You Are Given the Power to Close the Gap.

The challenge always resides in figuring out how you will bridge the gap. The first thing you want to do, using your analytical mind *and* your imagination is to picture yourself standing on the edge of the proverbial gap in your life. As you stand there and look across that divide, the first action is to recognize and accept responsibility for any-and-all choices and decisions you have made that contributed to the creation of this gap. *Response-ability* is your ability to respond to anything in life with the attitude of personal duty and a position of authority that is willing to take

191

ownership for the outcome in front of you. In taking responsibility for creating the gap, you are given the power to manage the gap, and to close the gap.

Accepting total responsibility for our past choices and decisions is also a great reminder that our power to choose and decide, is the brush that we use to paint each day of our lives. Accepting responsibility for our past allows us to tap into and fully own our power in the present. It's the realization that we are the artist of our lives. Capable of creating a masterpiece.

There is only space for one person in the driver's seat, at the steering wheel of your life, and that seat belongs to you. You may have heard that the definition of insanity is repeating the same thing over-and-over again but expecting a completely different result. If you want to experience things differently on the outside you must change things on the inside. One is a direct reflection of the other. When you alter the way you think, you will alter what you perceive, and when you alter your perception you will alter your choices and decisions. When you alter your choices and decisions, you alter your life.

Lead yourself to success. Taking full responsibility for your past, present and future is taking on a position of leadership. You take responsibility for leading *you*. John Maxwell is a leading authority on leadership and he teaches that the hardest form of leadership is self-leadership. The most difficult person to lead in your life is you. I would add that it's impossible to lead yourself without first placing responsibility on yourself. Self-accountability makes visible the pathway to self-leadership.

Gilbert Arland has been quoted many times for the following wisdom. When an archer misses the mark, he turns and looks for the fault within himself. Failure to hit the bullseye is never the fault of the target. To improve your aim, improve yourself. Along this same vein, I would also add that, in comparing the shooting of a bow, to the actions of your life. It's critical to keep your thinking arrows sharp and your aim responsibly focused.

3

Learn to Correct and Adjust

Things Change as Plans Unfold and You Must Be
Ready and Willing to Correct and Adjust

President Kennedy got the whole nation excited about a BIG dream. a dream to transport a man to the moon and bring him back home safe and sound. NASA carefully and meticulously mapped out the course of the journey. Covering every aspect from start to finish, down to the smallest detail.

In getting from where you are right now to where you want to be in the future, the quickest way to get there is a straight line. So, let's say the earth is point A and the moon is point B. Imagine a straight line angling upward from the earth to the moon, connecting the two points. Sort of like the backslash on your computer keyboard.

Thanks to all the state of the art advanced equipment that NASA had at its disposal, they knew exactly where the moon was. They had high-resolution photographic images taken by the Lunar Orbiter satellite and surveyor spacecraft. Tapping into all of their vast array of technologies, money and data, they were able to chart a straight-line course from the earth to the moon. Mission planners studied the lunar surface for two years figuring out the best place to land.

The Success of Their Mission Was Based on Their Ability to Correct and Adjust.

On July 16th 1969 at 9:32 EDT, Apollo 11 launched into space from Kennedy Space Center. They made a successful journey to the moon and back. After returning to earth, the team analyzed all the data and discovered that in getting from point A to point B, they were only on course 3% of the time. Meaning they were off course 97% of the time.

What this means is that the success of their mission was based on their ability to correct and adjust. That is how super achievers operate. They know that even the best laid plans are based solely on what they knew at the time the plans were created. Things change as plans unfold and we must be ready and willing to correct and adjust. This is how we avoid being put to far off course by other opportunities, challenges, distractions and detractors that are not in alignment with our purpose.

Correcting and adjusting is critical to success. Here is a great question to ask yourself. *Is what I'm thinking about doing, in alignment with my vision and my purpose and moving me in the direction of my end goal?* In other words, is the next action I'm considering, going to move me closer too, or further away from my ultimate-goal? This is how you sort through the mass of information, temptation, ideas and offerings that we are bombarded with every day.

If you make a choice or a decision, and later realize that it is leading you away from your vision and your purpose than its time to correct and adjust, to get back on course. Realize that if you raise your level of awareness through the practice of reflecting daily on the choices and decisions you have made; your inner guidance system will tell when you need to correct and adjust. As long as you know where your point A and your point B are located then you have a sense of direction. You know what your expectations are, based on your vision. Knowing all of that, it's important that you learn to trust your intuition and never hesitate to seek feedback from trusted sources.

4

Spend More Money on The Inside of

Your Head Then You Do on The Outside of Your Head?

Invest in Your Most Important Asset

We spend so much money on the outside of our head. I've seen people who have had so many facelifts that if they had one more they would literately go back in time. We spend well over seven hundred dollars a year on the outside of our heads. We spend money on things like tanning, grooming and even cosmetic surgery. Haircuts, make up, shampoo and conditioner. And that is just a partial list of the things we spend money on for the outside of our heads.

But the minute I ask someone to invest a little money on the inside of their head, on things such as a book, audio program, a workshop or a seminar for personal growth, all-of-a sudden, they think their head is not worth it.

What is wrong with this picture? It seems to me like we have this backwards, because if we took some of that money and spent it on the inside of our heads we would feel better on the inside. Our self-esteem would go up, our confidence would be greater. We would have better attitudes and a better outlook on life. We would develop greater habits and achieve greater things in life. We would feel so amazing on the inside that we would give off a natural organic radiating warmth, a blooming ray of light, a shimmering afterglow. It would emanate from our bodies and people would notice. If you did not spend one more penny on the outside of your head, people would still say you look great.

T.Harv Eker is the author of *Secrets of the Millionaire Mind*. He shares this with his audience; *If you want to change the fruits, you will first have to change the roots. If you want to change the visible, you must first change the invisible.* You are your

195

number one asset and your outside world will always be a reflection of your inner world. All meaningful and lasting change starts first on the inside, in your imagination and works its way out into your life. If you want to change what is going on in your outside world than your next step is invest on the inside of your number one greatest asset. YOU.

5

Set Your Worries Free

The More Time You Spend Visiting and Revisiting the Same Thought, the More Power You Give It

My experience from talking to people and listing to the conversations of others brought me to a conclusion that I later discovered was backed by research. One of the largest commonalities that much of the human populace shares, is a totally habitual mind trap that we too often get caught up in. It's the harmfully toxic habit of worrying. Leo Buscaglia has stated that *worry never robs tomorrow of its sorrow, it only saps today of its joy.*

I also discovered that worry is directly related to the lack of belief in your own faith. Faith doesn't work for you, it works through you. Faith believes in you and for it to work, you must believe in it. The smaller your faith, the greater your worries. If you worry too much, then *more faith* is just what the doctor ordered.

Faith is a knowledge within the heart that is beyond the reach of proof. You may say you have faith in the infinite power of God's universe, but do you still worry after asking for help? If so, then the message you are conveying is that you don't trust in the power you proclaim to believe in. Your level of faith is measured by your level of applied trust. If you lack trust and your ability to act on that trust, then you diminish your ability to receive.

Another important consideration is, when you devote your time to worrying about something, you are also devoting a substantial amount of energy from your mind and your body. Focusing all this combined energy to the thing you worry about is like feeding a beast. It makes it bigger and stronger.

Giving your worries increased levels of attention is much like soil and water to a seed or a plant, you only help it to grow. The more time you spend visiting and revisiting a thought, the more energy you give it. Energy flows where attention goes. And the more energy you give it, the more power you give it. The more you think about what you don't want, the greater your chances of getting more of, what you don't want.

Here Is the Key to Unlocking a Stress-Free Life

It's your thinking. What you think about, comes about! Creation is constant in our lives; Manifestation is ongoing. The fruit garden of your mind is always growing things. Take time and responsibility for weeding your garden. Weeds have roots too, and they can entangle with the roots of your fruits, resulting in the strangulation and subsequent death of your crops. Robbing you of your harvest. The question we must frequently ask ourselves is, *what am I creating?* When you give more attention and energy to the things you *do* want. You are simultaneously taking energy away from the things you *don't* want. Without energy to feed on, the weeds, things you *don't* want will essentially starve to death. Therefore, focusing on what you *do* want will reap a harvest that is far more beneficial to your health and your state of mind.

On a lighter note, you can always do what Mike the smart executive did. He hired a guy named Jerry to do all his worrying. One day he was telling his friend how great it was, not to worry about anything, and how refreshing it was to be living a stress-free life.

197

His friend thought that was an amazing idea, so he asked, how much is Jerry charging you for this service? And Mike said, nine hundred dollars a month. Wow! How on planet earth are you going to afford that said the friend? Mike smiled and replied, lucky for me, I don't have to worry about it. That's Jerry's job.

6

Impossible Means Possible

Impossible Is Not One Word! It Is Three Words

Anything is possible and everything is impossible. WAIT A MINUTE!!! How can everything be possible and impossible at the same time? Are you ready to break thru to new levels? Everything is possible and impossible at the same time because they are one in the same! Two seemingly different words that are both communicating the same meaning. I know, right now you may be thinking that I consumed large amounts of psychedelic drugs in my youth, but the truth is I have never consumed *any*.

You are going to experience a shift in your thinking right now that will change the way you think today, tomorrow and every day for as long-as you live. Do you know the difference between can't and can? The only difference is the letter "T" which stands for your thinking. If you look closely at the word *thinking* you will see that it is two words *thin* and *king*. Your thinking is either on the *thin* side or you think like a *king*, so how is it going? How is your "T" doing?

Scientists have proven beyond the shadow of a doubt, that darkness is a fallacy. Darkness does not exist, only varying degrees of light. And the scientific discovery most important to this segment is that weakness in the realm of human potential is also an utter fallacy. It is nonexistent, there are only *varying degrees of*

198

strength. Forget the word weakness, always think in terms of strength. When someone asks you, what is your biggest weakness, they are asking you for your smallest strength.

Staying inside the vein of personal growth and human potential, let me shine the spot light on what is perhaps the biggest misconception in our lives. There is no such thing as *impossible*. There is only *possible*. From now on I want you to think of possible and impossible as the same thing. Everything is possible and impossible at the same time, and in the same moment because they are the same thing. If you look closely at the word *impossible* you will see that it is an affirmation in the form of what is called an embedded command.

An example of an embedded command is; *can you tell me what you need before you will authorize an agreement between us*. It looks like a question, but it is an embedded command. If you remove the words *can you*, what you have left is the command - *Tell me what you need before you will authorize an agreement between us*. We dress it up to give it the appearance of a question, as not to offend the conscious mind or alert it to the reality that we are delivering a command to the subconscious mind.

Now, let's look again at the word impossible. I want you to write it down and look at it. Within the word impossible, you see the word possible. If the impossible is not possible than why do 80% of the letters in the word *impossible*, spell the word *possible?*
The answer is that it is what I call self-embedded command! Embedded commands are what you give other people. Self-embedded commands are what you give yourself.

From now on you look at the word impossible like this. Impossible is not one word! It is three words. **I-m-possible**, which is the same as saying *I am possible*. The self-embedded command within the word impossible is *I am Possible*! And that is the way you will read the word impossible for the rest of your life. Everything in regard to your success is *POSSIBLE*.

7

Para-Noia Will Destroy Ya and Pro-Noia Will Restore Ya

Optimist Prime

There is no future in the past. People who live there will die there, unless they get out and learn to live in the present. Even in the present we must strive to avoid negative thinking. Because making a habit of negative thinking creates ruts in the brain and the only difference between this sort of rut and a grave site are the dimensions. Zig Ziglar always referred to negative thinking as *stinkin-thinkin*. I have a solution to this problem, let me explain it to you.

I know people who are always looking on the bright side of things. The glass is always more than half full, it's overflowing. If someone gives them lemons, they make lemonade. I'm certain you're familiar with the sort of people I'm talking about. If the soles of their shoes wore completely through they would be excited because they were *back on their feet*. Speaking of feet, what about the boxer who spent so much time on his back when fighting in the in the ring, that he started selling advertising space on the bottom of his shoes. This kind of person thinks of problems as opportunities or what I call *problotunities*.

I have a nickname for these people that specialize in displaying enthusiastic optimism. I call them "*Optimist Prime.*" Because the word prime literally means; "*of the first, or greatest importance.*" In other words, Optimism is of the greatest significance, it is of the upmost importance in achieving the greatest levels of success.

Pronoia Will Restore Ya

200

Pronoia is another great word to put at the top of your list of words will use the most starting now. You have heard people say that *paranoia will destroy ya*. The opposite of that would *be Pronoia will restore ya*. The word *pronoia* is described as the opposite state of mind to paranoia. Pronoia is having the sense that the world is conspiring to help you. Many have leaned on the meaning of pronoia to define a philosophy that the planet was assembled to purposefully and secretly benefit those that choose to tap into its almighty capacity. A grand conspiracy to guide the individual towards success. This philosophy has been taught by many people such as Paul J. Meyer, Norman Vincent Peale, Napoleon Hill and many other classic educators of success principles.

W. Clement Stone, was often described as a reverted contrarian, or more commonly known in his language as an inverse paranoid. Instead of believing the entire planet was always fraudulently planning to conspire against him. He chose to believe the opposite. That the world had gathered its forces on his behalf and was continuously using those forces in his favor. His thoughts and emotions were harmoniously meshed to produce feelings that were always in support of his expectations. His expectations that the world was plotting to do great things for him and thus, great things were always in bloom.

To follow in Mr. Stone's footsteps will require you to practice holding the belief that when you regularly hold positive specific intentions, and strong expectations for your intentions to be fulfilled, you create the capacity for those great things to be attracted into your life. And you create the capacity to receive them. Instead of seeing a challenge as a negative, you see it as a haven for opportunities and you begin searching for them. Seek and you shall find.

Success would be a lot easier, and approach you at greater speeds if you were regularly expecting the world to advocate and promote your ambitions while eagerly supplying you with everything you need to accomplish your dreams. There is such an abundance of scientific and spiritual research supporting the almighty influence of intention and expectation, that the remarkable evidence of this ever-expanding truth has led many great leading authorities from past centuries and the present to declare intention and expectation universal laws of prosperity.

Here Are Some Common Traits of yourself living life as Optimist Prime.

- You know your *why*. Your purpose in life.
- You have a vision that is aligned with your purpose.
- You have goals that completely express your purpose and vision.
- Your Expanding your emotional intelligence (EQ)
- Your increasing your Self-confidence by increasing know how.
- Your Self-Esteem is a healthy, bright shining star.
- You look for opportunities in everything.
- You understand that *everything* matters.
- You Exercises daily, boosting activity in essential areas of the brain needed for things like learning and decision making.
- Your committed to life-long learning.
- You practice gratitude daily.
- You are action oriented.
- You take time for reflection.
- You meditate and quiet your mind daily.

And last but-not least Optimist Prime consistently uses the powerful forces of intention and expectation. The dominating personal vibrations of positive expectancy that successful people radiate, attracts to them like a magnet, the very experiences they created and held in their minds eye.

8

The Five People Principle

Who You See the Most Is Who You'll Be the Most

Jim Rohn was a motivational speaker and sensational self-help guru up until the time of his unfortunate passing. He said that *You are the average of the five people you spend the most time with.* I added a little something on the end, that I feel is crucial to success.

You are the average of the five people you spend the most time with. **including yourself.**

The people you spend the most time with influence your behaviors. Those people can elevate you or they can bring you down, it works both ways. The principle is a universal truth that can be your ally or your enemy.

The people you contribute the most time to will influence every aspect of your being at a subconscious level and even a cellular level, without you even realizing it's happening. It's effecting your language, the places where you spend time, the things you do, your hobbies, your habits, your spiritual nature, your level of consciousness and even your financial thermostat which determines how much money you will make.

If you add up the income of the 5-working people you contribute the most of your time to, and divide it by five, that is going to be about where your income level will be for the remainder of your life or until you decide to take-action and make some changes.

Some of the people you spend the most time with may not have an income therefore when I say add up the income, that implies that you're looking at the 5-*working* people that you spend the most time with. If they have no income than they can't contribute to the formula. Just for further clarification, when your considering your financial thermostat you want to look at the five-working people you spend the most time with. When we talk about language, habits, actions and everything else outside of finances, we are talking about the five people you spend the most time with weather they are working or not.

It's critical that you do some reflective thinking and examine this principle closely. Ask yourself what or who, you need to hang onto, and what or who, you would be better off letting go of. There could be a lot of potential inside of you that is not being released because it is all bottled up by the container you are currently living in. Your container is shaped by how you spend your time and who you share and entangle your time with. Let me illustrate this for you with a story about a farmer who took one of his pumpkins to the state fair and entered it into a contest for pumpkin growers.

The pumpkin was very unique, in that it was the exact size and shape of five-gallon jug, including the shape of the handle and mouth of the jug. As you can imagine, his entry turned out to be an award-winning pumpkin. He won a blue ribbon which means his pumpkin exceeded the standards set for his class, He also won a purple ribbon, meaning his exhibit was outstanding. One of the judges came by after the show and asked him how in the world he was able to grow a pumpkin that looked just like a five-gallon jug.

The farmer said *it was as easy as hanging out with my five best friends*. It took very little effort. It wasn't long after the seed was planted that it started to bloom. I put it inside of a five-gallon jug and watched it grow. After spending enough time inside the jug, it grew to be the exact shape and size of the five-gallon jug. Then I broke the glass and there it was. A perfect copy of the jug.

This is what we do with our lives. The five-gallon jug is like the five people we spend the most time with, in many ways we become like them. We take on the size and shape of their character, their dreams, their income and many other characteristics. My friend Brian Walsh is an expert in personal growth and in one of his books titled BRAINWIDTH, he states that *"Our social inter-*

204

actions carve out cognitive maps containing stereotypes, beliefs, fixed responses, attitudes and behavioral patterns. In terms of how your social plane effects your success, the richer the social network a person has the greater the person's success."

Another good friend of mine by the name of Joshua Schneider is the author of an excellent book called *GENERATION NEXTLEVEL* and in his book he uses the analogy that *"a tiny drop of red dye will turn a whole gallon of water pink. You just cannot escape the subtle influences that wield over you."*

The environment you live in which is essentially the people, places and things you surround yourself with is the absolute most critical aspect of success. Your outside influences move subtly through your conscious awareness. They can subtly wire themselves into your subconscious mind and they can also become rooted into your being at the cellular level, as powerful behavioral patterns without you even realizing that it's happening.

9

The Golf Ball Philosophy

When you change the way you look at something, the thing you look at changes. Try it.

When you look at a golf ball you notice all these tiny little indentations that create bumps all over the ball. Well that's not how golf balls started out. The bumps came about as a result of being knocked around over and over again. Back in the old days when golf balls were young and innocent they didn't have all these bumps. The coating on the ball was a smooth surface.

As the golfers used the same balls over and over again, the wear and tear left scratches, nicks and bumps all over the surface of the ball. Most golfers would then throw them away and get new balls. But the ones that kept the old balls and continued to use them made an amazing discovery.

What they noticed over time was that the more beat up the balls were, with all the scratches, nicks and bumps. The better their performance was. They actually flew truer and faster and farther than the brand-new balls with the smooth surface. Consequently, the used, beat up balls became standard use, golfers would use the new balls for practice and when they were sufficiently beat up and covered with bumps they would then use them in the tournaments.

As a result of this discovery, in 1905 a golf ball manufacturer name William Taylor became the first person to intentionally add bumps to his golf ball design. Today bumps are mandatory on the golf ball. On American golf balls, there are usually 336 bumps. Although some special types of balls can have as many as 500 bumps. The more bumps the better the performance.

THIS IS NOT ONLY TRUE IN GOLF; IT IS ALSO TRUE IN *YOUR* LIFE

All the bumps you have, the scratches, the scars, the bruises you have gotten over the years can actually make you fly truer, faster and farther in life and in business. Therefore, don't think about all those residual wounds and those emotional scars from your past as a bad thing. They are actually things that support you. Your past experiences have better equipped you to handle things in the future. You can tap into this belief if you haven't already and be a much bigger and stronger person on the inside as a result.

I mentioned earlier that some golfers chose to throw away the beat-up balls. They saw the scratches, dings and bumps as problems. Others decided to keep using the beat-up balls and discovered an opportunity that improved their performance and increased their success. ***Problems and opportunities*** *always coexist. That is why I deleted the word problem from my vocabulary. I put the words problem and opportunity together and made my own word that I feel is much more fitting of life. The word is PROBLOTUNITY.*

Calamity, challenges, misfortune, catastrophe, sorrow, hardship, difficulty, trouble, suffering, tough-luck, misery and more. There are lots of labels you can put on problems, but they can all be summed up into one word called *adversity. In every adversity, there are at least one or more equal or greater seeds of opportunity if we only give ourselves the faith and belief that they exist and give our eyes the desire to see them.*

My son Isaac loves big floor puzzles and we do them together often. Many of the puzzles are actually two puzzles in one. They have pictures on both sides and you can choose which one to put together. I remember this when I think of problems and opportunities, I think of one side of the puzzle as the problem and the other side as the opportunity. We can spend our time trying to figure out the problem side or we can flip all the pieces over and assemble the opportunity side. In the process of assembling the side with opportunities, guess what is happening to the problem side of the puzzle? The problem side of the puzzle is being solved as a result of our focusing on the opportunities. Too many people in business and in life, spend too much time focusing on what's wrong rather than focusing on what's right. If we spend more time looking at what's good and what's right we find that questions from the other side get answered, blanks get filled in, riddles get solved and new doorways are discovered.

The only difference between problems and opportunities is how you choose to look at them. The fact that problems and opportunities always coexist is one of the reasons why I love problems. I love problems because they always come baring gifts. Just like the golf ball did. Where there are problems, there are opportunities. They never come alone. They always come together. It may not be obvious, you may not see them holding hands, or hugging and kissing each other. They may not even be standing right next to each other. But they are never far apart. In

207

every problem or every adversity there is always, at least one or more equal or greater seeds of opportunity.

Different choices produce different results. When you change the way you look at something, the thing you look at changes. Let me say that again. *When you change the way you look at something, the thing you look at changes.* Only 4% of what we see actually comes through the eyes. The other 96% is a process of co-creation between the brain and the mind, using information from your other senses as well as memories of past experiences.

Therefore, you may see something as a problem and someone else may not see it that way. If you fill a glass with water to the half way mark, some people will be optimistic and tell you it's half full. Other people will be pessimistic and tell you that it's half empty. My question for you is; *Are those the only two possible answers?* Absolutely not. If you set that same half glass of water on the table in front of an engineer, a mathematician or a scientist and ask them if the glass is half full or half empty, their answer might be, *the glass is twice as big as it needs to be.* If you change the way you look at something, the thing you look at changes.

If you sat a half glass of water on the table in front of me and said. There are only two ways you can see this glass. You can see this glass as half full. Or you can see it as half empty. If you tell me it's half full, *you're an optimist.* If you tell me it's half empty, *you're a pessimist.* Now tell me. Which are you? An optimist or a pessimist?

I would look at the glass for a minute, pick it up, and drink the water. Then I would put the glass back on the table in front of you and say.

I'm a problem solver.

10

You Gotta Go More to See More

Low beams, high beams and the super bowl.

In business and in life the most important part of it is the part that is right in front of you. You don't have to be able to see all the way from Jackson Michigan to Long Beach California in order to drive there in the dark. On low beams your headlights light the way 250 feet at a time, as you move through that 250 feet another 250 is revealing itself.

If you stop you are limiting your vision to just the 250 feet in front of you, if you want to see more you have to go more. The only way to know what is farther down the road is to keep moving.

while some people are standing still, wondering if they should risk the next move, speculating about what may or may not lie ahead in the darkness, your headlights are filled with courage and your expectations are lighting the way. You move a little more, you see a little more, you move a lot more you see a lot more.

In life, every action taken initiates a feedback loop. The action goes out ahead of you, lighting the way and returning information by revealing more of what's in front of you, thus completing a feedback loop. This information gives you the power to correct and adjust and take the next action, starting the next loop with more wisdom and experience that keeps those lights shining brightly in front of you, revealing more and more information. Every action returns feedback that makes the next action more intelligent.

The size of the loop is determined by the size of your actions, if you drive with your low beams on your only seeing the next 250 feet but if you take more risk and flip on your high beams you initiate bigger loops, you see farther ahead and get back more information and bigger results.

With your high beams on you can see 350-500 feet ahead of you, that is approximately 100 to 166 yards, or one to one and a half football fields. As you can see, if you extend the size of your action, you extend the length of your vision.

Every pro football team dreams of winning the super bowl. They want to win the football super bowl, and you want to win the business super bowl, or the super bowl of life. How does a football team win a super bowl? Well, you can't win a super bowl unless you can get to the super bowl first and to do that you have to win enough playoff games. In order to get to the playoffs, you have to win enough regular season games and to do that you have to win one game at a time.

The only way to win a game is to score more points in each game than your opponent and how do you do that? You move the ball up field and to do that you need some first downs and to get first downs you have to grind out the yardage, one yard at a time. How do you get more yardage? You have to have a playbook. Any great playbook will tell you that the first order of business is to get a first down and take it one play at a time, initiating a play starts a loop and by the time that play is over you have gained feedback that helps you correct and adjust your strategy for the next play.

If you don't hike the ball, you got no play. The only way to win a game is to get in and play. Be willing to put in some sweat equity and do whatever it takes to succeed. Every time a team steps on the field they know that there is going to be a winner and there is going to be a loser but the team that wins is the team that steps on the field with the full intention and expectation of winning.

The team that makes the strongest commitment will not settle for anything less than a victory. They play smart and most of all, they keep playing, they hike the ball, they execute, they huddle to correct and adjust and plan the next play, then they hike the ball again. They win the game one play at a time.

Million Dollar Tip: sometimes things get foggy and you have a hard time seeing what's in front of you, the road may be revealing itself in much smaller increments. This can be uncomfortable but learn to make the uncomfortable comfortable. At one point or another most everything is born out of uncertainty, pay no mind to it, the great thing about fog is that it's always temporary, keep moving and you will move through it, and you will regain a clear view of what's ahead.

11

S.U.C.C.E.S.S FORMULA

Success is consistent daily incremental progress towards a worthwhile goal, long enough to produce the desired outcome.

As you may have noticed, I love acronyms because they are a great tool for breaking down a large chunk of information and tying it all together using the acronym. It's much easier to store and recall information when it's structured and built around an easy to remember acronym, and what better acronym for describing the instructions for success than the word S.U.C.C.E.S.S.

This model is perfect for your personal life and your business life, it is also a fantastic coaching tool for you to use in helping other people become successful. The two greatest leaders are, *students* who realize that they are also simultaneously leaders who teach others what they learn. And *leaders* who remember that they are also students who can learn from others of any walk or position in business or life. Here is a breakdown of the success formula.

Set SMART Goals
Understand your why

Current reality check
Choose your options
Establish your plan
Set your plan in motion
Stay on course

Now let's do a deeper dive and get a closer look at each part of the formula.

Set SMART Goals – Above every one of your smart goals you create to help take you from where you are to where you want to be, there must be a clearly defined purpose and a crystal-clear vision. Using the SMART GOAL TOOL Every goal you set will be molded and shaped to support and serve you when it's in alignment with your purpose and your vision. SMART is an acronym for;

Specific
Measurable
Attainable
Result Oriented
Time Specific

If your goal is not a smart goal, then it's not a goal.

SPECIFIC: Goals are no place to teeter totter. There is no room here to be fuzzy or unclear. Goals that are unclear are also uncertain. Obscure goals produce obscure results. Fragmented goals produce a fragmented future. Being clearly specific unleashes the power of our dreams and puts favorable forces into motion that send a clear message through vibrational frequency out into the universe, activating the process of manifestation that will return to you what you desire, through your actions. We are all broadcasting stations, sending out signals through our thoughts, intentions and expectations like the ones we are specific about in creating our goals. And we always receive a response back in the form of our results that is always a perfect match to what we have asked for. That is why we need to be very specific when setting goals. How we establish priorities and manage our time needs to be developed in favor of specific goals so that everything is in alignment and we achieve the results we expect.

MEASURABLE: Regarding your goals, if you can't measure them, you're wasting your time. Measuring allows you to correct and adjust to stay on track. What is the point in having a point A and a point B if you don't take time to chart your coarse. This is how you measure progress along the way, this is how you know when to correct and adjust, and this is how you know when you meet your goal. For example, a goal that states; *Go to the gym 5 times a week and exercise for one hour*, is much better than a goal that states; *lose weight and feel better*.

ATTAINABLE: There's a difference between setting goals that stretch you and goals that leave you disappointed. Goals are meant to stretch you and keep you focused. set short-term goals that you are realistic and attainable. These short-term goals will help keep you focused and moving toward your long-term goals. Setting goals that are too lofty or long-term can be demotivating. For example, run 100 miles in one year may sound a bit lofty but if you say, run 2 miles a week it sounds a lot more attainable. Giving yourself goals that are short-term, realistic and attainable makes it easier to believe in yourself and your ability accomplish your mission. Your belief is one of the critical aspects that drive you to maintain your pursuit of change and to reach the end goal.

REALISTIC: goals that are unattainable set you up to feel like a failure. For example, learn to ride a unicycle next week maybe completely unrealistic if you have never practiced a day in your life. I learned to ride a unicycle and I can testify that one week is not realistic. A more realistic goal might be to ride a unicycle in four months. This gives you plenty of time to practice and greatly improves your chances of success.

TIME SPECIFIC: A goal without a deadline is just a dream. Goals that are not time specific lack sense of urgency. It's important to be specific. You have a better chance of achieving a specific goal rather than a vague goal. For example, I'm going to lose 27lbs by May 10th, 2018 at 9pm is better than, *I'm going to lose weight this year*.

A goal is not a goal unless it has a beginning and an end. A starting line and a finish line. The brain is a goal-oriented mechanism just like the guidance system on a missile, it has to have the destination programmed so it knows where it's going. The same with your inner GPS system, it knows where you're at, but you have to give it the destination, so it can plan your route for you. It's the same way with your brain.

UNDERSTAND YOUR WHY: Below are three paramount reasons for understanding your why.

ONE: Goals get their shape, their focus and their direction from being aligned with a purpose and a vision. To set smart goals you must understand your why, which is your purpose. And you must have a vision of what the purpose is going to look like as it's being built and, what it's going to look like when it's finished. A clear understanding contributes feelings of confidence and a certainty to your faith, belief and desire.

TWO: Understanding a meaningful why, gives you strength to fight the pushback from your subconscious mind. Pushback occurs when you try to convince the subconscious mind to change its current image of reality to the new image of reality that you are going to create. The subconscious will fight you, and it will be a tug of war until the subconscious believes that the new image is the one you really want. That's why it's important to develop a burning desire for what you want. Whether you win or lose will be determined by your performance on the battlefield of the mind. Quitters never win, and winners never quit.

THREE: The achievement of your goal must benefit everyone it comes in contact with. Your success comes at nobody's expense. Nobody has to lose for you to win. No one else should ever be deprived as a result of your gain.

Understanding a genuine why will give strength and authentic-ity to your pursuit. Having and understanding a strong why is the bedrock of your goal setting process, it's the foundation that goals are built on.

CURRENT REALITY CHECK: There are two things you need to know in order be successful at any substantial endeavor. You need to know where you're at and you need to know where you're going. If you understand your why, and you have a clear purpose, vision and goals, then you know where you're going. A current reality check lets you know where you are right now. Your cur-rent position is going to be your starting point in the pursuit of your goals. The starting point needs to be accurate.

This step is critical, and it requires you to be brutally honest with yourself and your evaluation of your current reality. If you are not completely honest with yourself at this step, everything you do from here will be built on a lie.

CHOOSING YOUR OPTIONS: You created your S.M.A.R.T. Goals to help get you from where you are currently, to where you want to be. Between where you are now and where you want to be is a gap, reaching your goal requires you to close that gap. In this step, you conduct a gap analysis. A gap analysis can be done for either personal development or business development.
An honest gap analysis will give you a sense of direction and give you a way to measure the proficiency of your future decisions and actions. It's a simple way to help individuals as well as businesses achieve their goals and objectives. In a nutshell, a gap analysis is a process that helps you bring together your actual reality with your desired outcome. It enables you to find ways to bridge the gap between your current reality and your goal by establishing the best objectives. Your objectives are the stepping stones on your road map to success. The best way to start your gap analysis is by presenting yourself two questions.

- The first question is; *Where are you now? (Your current reality)* and the second question is;

215

- Where do you want to be? (*Your smart goal*)

The process of writing down detailed answers to these questions will enable you to develop a properly aligned and realistic plan of action and give you a clear estimation of the distance between where you are and where you want be. Write down all the ideas you can come up with for closing the gap and reaching your goal. Then choose the ones that will best serve as the objectives to start moving you in the direction of your goals. These choices and decisions are the material you will use in the next step to build your plan of action.

ESTABLISH PLAN: From your list of choices you begin developing your plan of action. The process of establishing your plan may trigger additional ideas that you did not think of when you were brain storming your list of possible options. One quality of successful people is to remain flexible. Regardless of how great you think your plan is, it will most likely change when you put it into action, because action brings you feedback through its results and that information will help determine if you need to make corrections and or adjustments to the next planned action. Create a plan that makes the most sense and respond accordingly as the plan unfolds and reveals new information.

Million-Dollar Tip*: Eliminate distractions and detractors.*

SET YOUR PLAN IN MOTION: Take action. The only way to translate a new vision and it's supporting goals into a new reality is by taking daily actions on a consistent basis long enough to produce results. Forget about having all the answers to every question. Begin where you are, with what you have, and start unfolding your plan. Action brings feedback and feedback returns wisdom that you need to make your next action more intelligent. Feedback will fill in the blanks and answer questions along the way. Be a cliff jumper and build your wings on the way down.

STAY ON COURSE: Even with the best plans, you will still have to correct and adjust. Remember, when NASA launches a spaceship to the moon, it leaves the launch pad with a flight plan programmed into the onboard navigation system. But they still need a room full of people sitting in the command center in Houston Texas to monitor the progress of the plan and help make corrections and adjustments as needed. During the first flight to the moon the space shuttle was on course 3% of the time meaning it was off course 97% of the time. This means that the success of the mission was totally dependent on the team's ability to keep correcting and adjusting.

12

Your Inner G-Me-S System

How we get from where you are to where you want to be.

Your Inner G-me-S, Global Me System is sort of like a GPS or Global Positioning System. The process of getting from where you are right now to where you want to be in the future is like using the GPS technology in your vehicle, or on your cell phone or tablet. For the GPS service to work it needs to know two things, where you are right now and where you want to go.

The navigation system receives signals from multiple satellites that triangulate your position and pin point where you are right now. When you type in your destination the navigational system creates a roadmap that displays the route you will take to your destination and all you have to do is follow the instructions.

Success in life works the same way, all you have to do is decide where you want to go via clarification of your vision. Then start driving towards your end goal using the objectives or stepping stones in between that the GPS refers to as your navigational instructions. The more the gap between here and there closes, the closer you get to your end goal. Accelerate forward using affirmations and visualization. Your inner G-me-S will continue to unfold your route as you progress. In other words, once you clarify and stay focused on your vision, holding it in your mind's eye, the next steps will keep appearing ahead of you along the way, just like your GPS does.

Life with no destination in mind is like the Wi-Fi on your smart phone, it will keep searching and searching until it finds a source that can supply it with what it needs. Your mind works the same way, it is a goal seeking mechanism and without some place to go it just keeps searching and searching, burning up your energy. Or even worse your subconscious mind will set goals for you without your conscious permission, often times based off old behavior patterns or old programs that you no longer wish to operate from. The only way you are going to be in control is to use your G-me-S System and monitor it to make sure that it stays on course.

You're G-Me-S system is designed to help you navigate and reach your destination, it is beneficial to all that use it. Unfortunately, a GPS and the G-me-S do not tell you when there will be rough terrain, detours, road blocks, areas that are being worked on, or bumps in the road. All this means is that from time to time you may need to reevaluate your route and determine whether-or-not to stick with the route you're on or take an alternate route that gets you to your predetermined destination.

My END and your NEW BIGINNING

The full book will be released in May 2018

Success **YOU**niversity

A Master Class in Personal Power.

Read more success strategies and leadership principles
on Daniel's blog at www.DanielGleed.com

Daniel's books are available around the world in multiple languages. They are available off line in your brick and mortar retails stores and online book stores such as Amazon.

Quantity discounts are available when ordering more than 25 copies. You can reach Daniel through his website.

Daniel is a John Maxwell certified team member, leadership coach, success coach, and trainer.

Daniel is also a certified trainer for the Nick Vujicic, YOUTHMAX PLUS program for kids and teens. Find out more at DanielGleed.com

To stay in the loop on Daniel's workshops, seminars, speaking engagements, book releases and training tools, you can connect with him on Pinterest, Google+, LinkedIn, Facebook, Twitter, Instagram, and his blog at Daniel Gleed.com

About the Author

Daniel Gleed is a success coach to the international community. He is known for his unique brand of street smart business savvy, strategic intellect, and his unique formulas for success. He loves helping people in Business and in life discover their next level, and he loves it even more when they are looking at their next level in the rear-view mirror. Living on the edge of their current potential and continuing to push their perceived boundaries until they discover that the only real limitations we have are the ones we place on ourselves by believing they exist.

Daniel teaches that failure is just feedback and he has failed his way to success. He is an award-winning speaker and his experience makes him uniquely qualified to talk about success using a magical mix of his humor, stories and wisdom that contribute to the personal style he deploys in keeping his audiences spellbound.

Daniel has studied and shared what makes successful people different. He knows what motivates them and what drives them. He is delivering this critical insight to countless people and audiences, sharing his success strategies with individuals, companies, and professional associations.

www.ingramcontent.com/pod-product-compliance
Lightning Source LLC
Chambersburg PA
BHW031954190326
20CB00007B/246